HEALING
IS THE
REVOLUTION

HEALING
IS THE
REVOLUTION

DENESE SHERVINGTON, MD, MPH

Published by
Institute of Women & Ethnic Studies
New Orleans, LA

Institute of Women & Ethnic Studies
365 Canal Street, Suite 1550
New Orleans, LA 70130

Acknowledgements

Penning *Healing is the Revolution* has been a labor of patience, humility, and love.

To the thousands of patients I have seen over the years, from those who were in psychotic crises in emergency rooms and inpatient units to the worried well in office-based outpatient therapy, for those who entrusted me with the interiority of your being—it has indeed been an honor. Thank you for being a teacher more powerful than any psychiatric text I have ever read!

And for those who have been part of the IWES family over the past 25 years, thank you for teaching me how to become a better leader and team player. Please know that as flawed as I have been at times in my delivery, my intent has always been to be transformative and adaptive. Love, compassion, and respect for our shared humanity and dignity have always been my guiding principles.

And for those who have allowed me the space of intimate love—my late husband, our two children, and my current partner, thanks for making my soul sing.

And finally, thanks to my amazing editor. Though you felt you were just doing your job and did not need acknowledgement, this would not have been possible without you.

This book is dedicated foremost to my two amazing grandbabies–Ayelet and Hadassah, thanks for reminding me once again of the joy of holding, nurturing, and lovingly attaching to the young spirit. This book is aimed at breaking the cycle of intergenerational trauma that could end up in your life and derail you from your journey to liberation and freedom.

In peace,

Denese Shervington MD, MPH

INTRODUCTION

> When you are inspired by some great purpose, some extraordinary project, all of your thoughts break their bonds. Your mind transcends limitations; your consciousness expands in every direction; and you find yourself in a new, great and wonderful world. Dormant forces, faculties and talents become alive and you discover yourself to be a greater person than you ever dreamed yourself to be.
> ~ Patanjali

At the tender age of seventeen I migrated from Jamaica, my birthplace, to the United States. After completing college and medical school in New York, I returned home with the intention of continuing my post-graduate medical education in surgery at the University of the West Indies. After six weeks of being home, I went to an Independence Day celebration in the town square. The local Jamaicans were exuberant and filled with pride; all except me. I did not feel connected to all the merriment happening around me. In that moment, I realized that I yearned to return to the life I had created in the US and the people whom I had come to love. I particularly missed my very dearest best friend and confidante, whom I had met in medical school.

A few weeks later, still feeling unsettled, the late great reggae singer Jacob Miller invited me to accompany him to visit a friend who lived a few houses down from my apartment. His friend turned out to be the Honorable Robert Nesta Marley, who by then had become a global superstar. Mr. Marley greeted us under a big shady tree at the side of his house which, I later found out, was where he regularly held court. When I shook his hand, he looked me up and down and remarked, "Rasta don't like when women show their legs." I was wearing shorts. In spite of feeling a bit miffed and flabbergasted at the patriarchal statement, I immediately obliged, rushed back home, and changed into a long skirt.

Normally I would have been angered by what seemed to be a misogynistic demand, and would have left, never to return. Especially since I was deeply ensconced in my newly emerging radical Black feminist identity and quest for gender equity. However, somewhere in my collective unconscious, like many others who visited regularly and hung on his every word, I intuited that I was in the presence of divine greatness. This was not a battle but an opportunity. From then on, appropriately dressed for being in his presence, I would join Jacob and the others gathered under the tree to revel in the pure poetry, philosophical wisdom, and reasoning that spewed forth from Bob Marley's lips, all the while he dribbled his football and smoked a spliff.

During these gatherings Bob Marley rarely spoke to anyone directly or in a personal way. However, one day, in his usual simple intensity, he once again looked me up and down as if studying me closely. I was properly fully clothed, but this time he was probing beyond the surface and instead assessing my mental wardrobe. As if feeling the discord within me, he simply said, "Go heal the people of I-thiopia (Ethiopia)." A humbling heaviness descended upon me, as a myriad of conflicting feelings flowed through me all at once—joy, excitement, exuberance, and dread. His directive seemed like spiritual guidance and validated my desire to become a more global citizen. It was the answer to the questions my restless soul had been asking while I aimlessly walked around my homeland, feeling like I was looking in from the outside.

A few weeks later, the universe provided the path that influenced my life in so many ways, personally and professionally. Where better to do so than in the city of the angels! A colleague assisted me in obtaining an internship in Family Medicine at a hospital in Los Angeles, the city where my best friend lived. A year later I met my husband and moved to San Francisco, where I completed my residency in Psychiatry at the University of California San Francisco. Finally, Bob's message that you can't run away from yourself came home to roost. Clearly, I had to take a detour back to my homeland to begin to answer the question, "Why am I here; what is my true purpose?" It has gradually become clearer to me that helping to heal the mental wounds of my people of the African diaspora is that which gives meaning to my existence.

During my early years of psychiatric training, two very powerful experiences would significantly shape my clinical career. The first was with a fourteen-year-old girl (whom I will refer to as YD) at a residential group home in Richmond, CA. She had been transferred to the group home from a hospital where she had undergone abdominal surgery for stab wounds inflicted by her alcoholic father. He had also been repeatedly subjecting YD and her siblings to sexual abuse. On the day he stabbed her, she attempted to run away with her younger brother after her father tried to force both of them into having group sex with him.

When YD arrived at the group home, she was severely regressed and depressed. She oftentimes refused to eat, spoke only very sparingly, and oftentimes acted like a non-verbal infant. After two years of intensive therapy in a milieu that tried to provide her with nurturing and corrective parental experiences, which at times required feeding her with a baby bottle, she began to improve. But shortly into this early stage of healing, YD's father hunted her down and began sending her letters begging for forgiveness, and inveigling her to move to Virginia, where he had begun a new life as a preacher. The letters were very upsetting to YD. Very soon thereafter, her behaviors began to regress; most notably she got increasingly hypersexual. Unfortunately, I had to discontinue being her doctor because my residency training ended and I had to move to a new position.

Months later I got a call at 2 a.m. from a friend who was an ophthalmologist. He told me he had just completed eye surgery on a young woman who kept muttering my name as she was coming out of anesthesia in the recovery room. She had been taken to the emergency room after she was found lying on the streets of Richmond, severely beaten and unconscious. She was in such bad shape my friend was only able to save one of her eyes. I rushed to the hospital. I will never forget the image of YD lying in the bed with her head and face bandaged. Her spirit was as broken as her bones. Her soul was as enucleated as her left eye.

YD shared with me that she had run away from the group home and had been living with an older john while she worked the streets. Her injuries were the result of one of her "tricks" getting angry and beating her. She was sure he hadn't expected her to survive. I held her and sobbed as she told me her story. It was the first time I ever let down my doctor patient boundaries. She felt ashamed and apologized for letting me down. But I too was ashamed, feeling I had abandoned her. I cried for her and for all young girls unable to protect themselves from the savagery of men who prey on them. I remember being very angry with her father for having placed her in his bed, from which she turned to the streets and to her downward spiral.

The other case was that of a fifteen-year-old male (MM) in juvenile detention. He was accused of driving the getaway car (his family's Rolls Royce) from an armed robbery, and was being held on charges of accessory to murder. I saw him daily while he awaited learning whether or not he would be tried as an adult. MM is one of those cases that seems to make no sense from the outside. MM had grown up in an extremely privileged Black household. He had been sent to private white boarding schools all his life. But, as is often the case, when he entered adolescence his previous white friends and their families began to shun him and avoid socializing with him.

So when he returned home the summer he turned fifteen, he literally went across the tracks in search of his Black male identity. He began to hang out with "real Black people," other young men in the hood. MM began to engage in what had been portrayed to him and what he identified as normative Black behavior—being a criminal. When he was arrested, in spite of all his family's wealth and social capital, his attorney was unable to keep him in the juvenile justice system; he was tried as an adult. When the ruling was announced, I once again broke down and cried—for him, for my children, for all the Black children, and all of the diaspora.

What these two cases taught me early in my career was that the marginality of gender and race imposed upon women and men of color render people of color very vulnerable to external traumatic forces. The global geopolitical system is built on racism and patriarchy; only whiteness and maleness serve as protective buffers. Hence, in addition to my later ambitions in academic psychiatry and population mental health, I continually honed my clinical skills as a racial- and gender-healing practitioner.

I am very fortunate that my training to become a psychiatrist occurred during the era when being a competent psychotherapist was as important as psychopharmacologic/medication management. Additionally, over the past thirty years I have pushed the boundaries of western mental health to incorporate those eastern, African, and indigenous practices that complement the attainment of bio-psychosocial and spiritual healing. Along this pathway I have studied acupuncture as part of traditional Chinese medicine, Buddhist mindfulness and compassionate practices, and the spiritual retentions in the African diaspora.

By integrating global healing science and wisdom, my tool-kit for prying open and unlocking our capacity for recovery, healing, and transcendence has expanded. I feel more capable of offering a comprehensive and holistic approach that can assist individuals in counteracting the sexist and racist forces that they encounter. I have accomplished this primarily using reflective uncovering psychothera-peutic practices and witnessing contemplative techniques that facilitate the process of self-awareness. And, when needed, I have supplemented these talking therapeutic approaches with adjunctive psychopharmacology and/or acupuncture.

Being an effective Black woman psychiatrist has meant that in the analysis of my patients' circumstances, I have had to center the experiences of race, gender, and class and how they intersect and create traumas for my patients. I have also had to be keenly aware of my own vulnerabilities, to avoid interjecting my own experiences into the therapeutic interface. As a Black woman, I can truly relate to gender and racial micro-aggressions. Indeed, I know what it feels like to enter a room of whiteness and be made to feel totally invisible, worthless, as if I do not exist. I also know what it's like to be cornered by wretched men and have them give such menacing looks that I feel violated and fear that they could harm or kill me. And I know what it means to be poor, having grown up in the racialized lower class in colonized Jamaica.

The positive upshot, however, is that my familiarity with patriarchy and racism has given me the advantage of being able to offer my Black patients a safe, relatable, and empathic mirror through which they can catch a glimpse of the tortured spaces that they have hidden from themselves and others. In so doing, I can become a safe container to help to bind their anxieties as they uncover those dark and terrifying places. We then explore and acknowledge the damage to their self-esteem, self-worth, and confidence. And after my patients have sat sufficiently with the pain, have gone to the edge and released the suffering, they can discover and try on new ways to call forth their less wounded selves and move closer to whom they truly are. In other words, by my being able to contain and hold the context of Blackness and womanhood, and model through my own ongoing healing process a way forward, my patients can feel hopeful about their own ability to unleash their way forward. Ultimately, my aim is to expand, not shrink, my patients' conscious awareness of their authentic selves.

From 1990 to 2003 I lived in New Orleans and raised our two children with my late husband, who passed away in 2000. When Hurricane Katrina devastated New Orleans in 2005, I was living in New York. I commuted back and forth between the two cities to render service in whatever way I could to ease the pain of people who had lost over eighty percent of their city and come face to face with death and dying. For the Black community, which suffered the most devastation and was the least supported, the trauma of the losses and disappearances (kinship ties and ancestral lineage) was extremely catastrophic.

I agonized for two years about leaving New York, mostly because the majority of my family live on the Northeast coast and also because I did not want to abandon my small cadre of private patients. The suffering of the people of New Orleans, especially Black children living in poverty, eventually got to me, and in 2008 I made the painful decision to return permanently to New Orleans. There I created a division of post-disaster mental health at the Institute of Women and Ethnic Studies (IWES), a translational, community-based public health organization that I founded in 1993.

My New York clients were not happy about my decision. I worried that I was abandoning them. Through much meditation, I came to accept that I was being called to pursue a higher purpose. Deep within I knew my painful decision was the one I had been destined to make—New Orleans was the physical space of, as well as the metaphor for, the I-tiopia that Bob Marley commanded me to heal!

And as much as I would miss the allure of living in the greatest city in the world, I took solace in returning to the community that had opened her arms and embraced my family and me. This was the city I had grown to love so dearly and where I raised my family. This was where my husband took his last breath. New Orleans needed me to return and give all that I could to help my people heal in the face of their humanity being once again desecrated. Black New Orleanians had been abandoned, many left to die in the storm, and, for those remaining, many left to suffer in the recovery. A little voice in me kept whispering, "you have a once in a lifetime opportunity to be part of a whole city's recovery and healing."

Over time, my New York clients, some of whom I still stay in touch with, understood the need for my move. In New Orleans, I am now referred to as the community psychiatrist, called upon by community members when they are in crisis and need to see someone they trust. For those who cannot afford to pay I lovingly offer my service for free. There is no greater honor in life! For the twelve years since Hurricane Katrina I have engaged in conceptualizing and implementing community and population level trauma-based services—wisdom circles, psycho-educational support groups, and existential work groups with thousands of Black women, men and youth.

In 2010, I spearheaded a yearlong project with Chaka Khan and her foundation to assist 50 local Black women in setting life goals. I conducted a monthly support group with the women to help them better understand their psychological make-up in order to create the psychological resilience they needed to pursue these goals. For many, this was the first time they had prioritized their emotional wellbeing. At the end of the program, the women reported increased self-confidence and self-esteem, and all had achieved at least one of their goals. Curious to pursue and more deeply interrogate the root cause of some of the self-negating cultural norms the women had identified, I partnered with the Anna Julia Center (founded by Dr. Melissa Harris Perry) to conduct Wisdom Circles and learn from Black women how they experienced their Blackness, their resilience, and their citizenship. Seventy Black women and men participated in this yearlong project in 2013. The findings, compiled by IWES in the booklet "Crooked Room: Stories from New Orleans" validated what most of us have experienced but which so many of us have tried to repress: that white supremacy ravages Black people's sense of wholeness, worth, value, and belonging, which can lead to the internalization of self-hatred and feelings of Black inferiority. As one participant stated, "I'm always a little crooked. Standing straight in a crooked room that someone else has constructed for you is close to impossible."

The lessons learned from these two projects have fueled my determination to write *Healing is the Revolution* and map out for us a pathway to our mental liberation. In addition, the recent events that have birthed a new iteration of a Black Lives Matter movement have also contributed to my sense of urgency for our redemption. Anti-Blackness institutional injustices and inequities have become almost unbearable, and have forced another crop of courageous Black beings to put their bodies on the line for freedom. This is the new and present day version of the same old collective psychic trauma that Black minds have suffered.

State-sponsored violence continues to take the lives of many unarmed Black people. Previously often experienced in isolated communities and hidden away from public detection, technology has now heightened our capacity to visually experience state-sanctioned murder of Black people. Black communities are now being validated when they speak of long standing institutional oppression. People in unaffected communities can less turn a blind eye to the obvious patterns of the defenselessness of the victims and the lack of just legal redress for the families. It is a bittersweet validation for Black people that there is public awareness now of their long being under unending siege, over-policed, and unprotected.

In addition, state-sponsored under- and mis-education of economically disadvantaged and resourced Black children has killed many dreams of socio-economic mobility. Black people in New Orleans were deemed refugees and criminals and left to drown during Hurricane Katrina. Black people in Flint are slowly being murdered by state-sponsored poisoned water. The hopeful promise of the civil rights era and integration is quickly fading. All of this has reignited another cycle of Black pain, shame, anger, and rage; heaped on top of chronic toxic adversity. The individual process of healing does not supplant the important need for the systems of brutal oppression to be dismantled and destroyed. It is part of the compendium of total Self and collective liberation.

We are in need of healing. The uncloaking of the injustices that we still face daily in the modern United States 150-plus years post slavery is a heavy burden, one made up of the still-present chains of slavery, the invisible bonds of poverty, and daily experiences of racism. We are hurt, we are angry; some of us are ashamed. Rather than merely being a validation of what many of us knew deep inside, this unmasking of present day racism is causing many of us to lose hope. The continuous, persistent oppression, bullying, and dehumanization can eventually lead to varying degrees of traumatic psychic injury. When turned inwards, that gets expressed along the depressive and/or anxiety continuum, or escaped through mind-numbing drugs or other unhealthy addictions to food and sex. Existentialist psychologist Rollo May argued that when people do not feel their significance and their agency, they become apathetic and then violent because humans cannot stand the "perpetually numbing experience of their own powerlessness." In other words, for some, when the trauma of dehumanization is directed outwards, it is often expressed along the behaviorally aggressive and violent continuum.

This climate of escalating injury therefore begs urgent interrogation on how to resist, heal, and grow from the ongoing threats to our mental well-being. The mind animates our experience of being alive. Without a healthily functioning mind, it is hard to live fully and joyfully. How do we therefore emancipate ourselves from mental bondage? For, as history continues to show, no one is coming to save us. The burden lies solely upon our mental agility and capacity for resilience. The questions become:

- How do we tap into our individual and collective efficacy?—"I can, and together we will."
- How do we heal our wounded hearts so that we can continue to create Black love and joy, and in so doing create caring communities for our children and the next generation?
- How do we honor and take better care of our bodies so as to live healthier and longer lives?
- How do we not slip into existential despair, and instead fully occupy our beings in the journey from birth to death?
- How do we dance within the mystery that is our human creation, so as to discover our purpose and meaning in life?

Healing is the Revolution presents a roadmap to healing. My thirty years of academic and public health experience, plus all the knowledge I have gleaned from my freedom-seeking clients in my clinical practice, has taught me that healing can be narrowed down to a fourfold process:

- Naming, noticing, and owning our injury
- Sitting with and understanding/discovering how injury has manifested in our mind, body, and soul
- Releasing our wounded-ness and suffering
- Creating and practicing new ways of being whole and healthy

Healing the wounded Black Self is not just an individual endeavor, however. Collectively, we have to continue to dismantle and disrupt the evil forces of Babylon that continue to oppress us and add extra layers of suffering to our existence.

In *Healing is the Revolution,* I draw upon my childhood dance through nature that growing up in the unspeakable beauty of Jamaica bestowed upon me. Many moments of inspiration during my penning oftentimes occurred during my early morning jogging meditations, listening to the wisdom of Robert Nesta Marley's teachings in his music. *Healing is the Revolution* is part of my humble response to his charge that I become a healer for my people and help us "rid ourselves from mental slavery for none but ourselves can free our minds." And finally, I draw upon the wisdom of other Black scholars, philosophers, and poets. It would be foolish of me to think that my voice alone can offer a complete pathway toward healing. I can only add another stream to the many tributaries joining the river that delivers us to the healing arms of Yemaja in the sea.

Healing is the Revolution is for all Black people who are ready to sing along with the Prophet, "Slave driver, the tables have turned." It begins with making the case for why we need healing then journeying through the injuries endured from slavery through to present day institutional inequities and injustices. The chapters that follow those lay out a healing pathway: psychotherapy, creativity, ancestral reverence, ritual and magic making, play, rest, and becoming centered in nature.

There is also a chapter on contemplative practices that ends with a section on an imaginal journey in search of Black mind redemption. Given that the present day world leadership is showing a significant imbalance of yin/yang energy, this imaginal journey is created in the metaphysical spirit of the feminine. The current destructive masculine yang energy is overpowering the creative and nurturing yin female energy, and this deficiency needs to be replenished if the planet is to be saved. We must let go of an Afro-enslaved past that has been peppered with inhumane and brutal patriarchal evil, and instead radically imagine an Afro-future graced with the feminine empress, the universal Yin, the source of a loving mother divine.

The once enslaved are finally now seeking an end to our bondage, external and internal. We are claiming a permanent solution to our freedom and liberation of the planet from the belief in a hierarchy of human value. May the revolution, which is our healing and liberation, serve as the vehicle for transformation!

Much respect,
Denese O. Shervington MD, MPH

Chapter 1

> The wretch that was burnt was made to sit on the ground, and his body being chained to an iron stake, the fire was applied to his feet. He uttered not a groan, and saw his legs reduced to ashes with the utmost firmness and composure.
> ~ Thomas Thistlewood

Many Black people, and some Whites, upon sitting through the depiction of horrors in the 2014 movie *Twelve Years a Slave*, were visibly shaken and sickened to their core. Torture. Forced breeding. Rape. Murder. The movie depicted but some of the inhumane conditions to which African slaves were subjected. So brutal and debased is this history that many would like to forget, some deny, others avoid. In the face of the graphic, historical evidence displayed on screen, there were those who expressed much cynicism and denial, "Why can't we just get over it and get on with our lives? Slavery has long been over!" What a psychic luxury it would be to do so!

The system of slavery may be over, but the ill effects of its 254 years of existence are still being unleashed on us through institutionalized and structural injustices. This harm is trapped within each and every one of us and is compounded by the modern day system that grew out of slavery. As such, this journey toward healing the injury necessitates an examination of how and why we are entrenched in this current day pathos of being oppressed and having to continuously prove that we're being oppressed, all while struggling to get support to change the unjust dynamics. Until we fully identify and acknowledge the lingering existence of slavery's effects on all of us—those who resist whole-heartedly as well as those of us who have adopted a multitude of self-harming habits to escape the brutality of our injuries—we will continue to have our lives and communities burdened by the symptoms of slavery.

White supremacy was the precursor and architect of the brutality of the transatlantic slave system. For centuries during and post slavery, the false premise that pronounced the white race superior and all others inferior created a hierarchy, an omnipresent caste system, which dehumanized all others at the expense of the white race's need to feel superior. This caste system continues to exist in present day, structurally and fundamentally, in our societal organization. Its form of expression may have changed, but its damage remains constant—inferiorizing, debasing, demeaning, devaluing, denigrating, terrorizing, and destroying Black lives.

Over time in American post slavery history, there was a cultural shift and public social intolerance for blatant racist behavior and overt racist language emerged. But with the base premise of the national institution unchanged, publicly stated opinions decrying discrimination and racism languished at the surface level. The efforts by minority groups with limited power, toothless laws that were marginally enforced, and agencies unwilling to rock the boat did not make more than a dent in the eradication of prevailing actions, perceptions, and stereotypes. Those were left unchecked, out of sight and mind, where they flourished and became more entrenched. In reality, the overall effect made it harder for Black people to name what it was that continued to cause us harm.

Instead of seeing bold strokes of oppression hard for anyone to deny, as part of our daily lives we encountered countless instances where our experiences of racism were downplayed and brushed aside as issues stemming from one or two bad apples. In the rush to "get over slavery already," what has not been probed is that these incidences are made up of both overt and passive acceptance of the white supremacist status quo. Black people in modern society are as damaged by those who fire a bullet, as by those who question, "Was he really being racist when he fired the bullet?" Or those who swear, "Well I would never have fired that bullet so don't look at me." Dodging the responsibility to engage when concerns were raised, casting doubt on a Black person's perception of racism, being unwilling to call out instances of racism experienced helps everyone duck the discomfort and anxiety that arises when discrimination and oppression are discussed.

Additionally, with crass racist language and overt hate actions being frowned upon, a sinister form of race-based micro and macro aggression in the form of denigrating language stereotypes became entrenched. Racist or discriminatory actions that had been driven beneath the surface reemerged as coded language: gestures, signs, and symbols that indicate difference. Terms such as "thug," "ghetto," "hood," "sketchy," and "shady" are all examples of this coded talk that is used to refer to or speak of Blackness without overtly sounding racially prejudiced.

And then, in a seeming backlash to the injury of seeing a Black man elected as head of the country, the dams burst and obvious, above board actions that once were easily identified as hateful and harmful became badges of honor amongst those who had long stewed in anger at racial gains achieved by Blacks. Hoods came off in exchange for chinos and polo shirts, and incels and white supremacists incredulously once again have become part of the everyday experience of Black living in the United States! Whatever progress we had achieved in feeling equity and as stakeholders in this country has been exposed as mostly a construct of everyone's "get over slavery" mindset, and not a true consequence of real healing and societal change.

As the wheels of time seem to be slipping back into a period we thought already conquered, technology has provided an unexpected assist in the resistance. Without a doubt the proliferation of social media has lit a fire under many once private, anonymous even, fringe groups. In current day America, they boldly no longer hide their racism and have unleashed a war of hatred and misinformation to rile up their masses. On the flip side, social media has also satiated the passive apologists who want to believe that retweeting a positive statement is tantamount to doing their part to counteract injustices.

But social media has also played an incredibly invaluable role in riling up public choruses of support and acknowledgment that Black people had no access to as they suffered the pain of micro aggressions or systematic abuses in isolated situations. Over the last several years, business as usual events to us (Black people), but astonishing to many other races who had previously dismissed our complaints as exaggerations, "that would never happen in these days and times!" have been documented and shared via social networking sites that shed light on the true inequality of Black existence in this country.

Some of these events captured on video are nonviolent but provocative, upsetting cases of neighbors policing Black people for a whole range of normal activities. Others have put the extremely critical, scary, and alarming frequency of unarmed Black males being killed by law enforcement agents on everyone's mobile phone and computer monitor. In the "one person's word against another" environment where the Black voice regularly got drowned out, social media has raised a cacophony of voices of support, created awareness, and sometimes sparked access to power that Black people did not have a chance of accessing before.

These deaths and other atrocities have generated outrage across communities looking for justice and accountability of law enforcement's excessive force when dealing with Black people. Some of us have angrily focused on the present circumstance around Black men being cut down; however, for others, these highly public cases also trigger our anger, vulnerability, and frustration, pent up from our dealings with various other oppressive institutions in our country. Our less easily documented instances of being whipped by the system resonate with the obvious examples of our being destroyed by stereotyping, trigger-happy white fingers. And while it has opened the eyes of many and begun to show slivers of change in some attitudes towards the prosecution of these cases—even if not yet being able to eliminate their frequency—the pushback has been similar to everything else we have seen before.

Sadly, law enforcement, the media, and other government voices have traditionally aggressively employed the defensive stance of recasting Black men as less than. Inevitably, the Black males who are killed by law enforcement have had their characters dissected and ultimately turned into "thugs" (the modern day "brute"), in an attempt to justify their death or to show personal contribution to their demise. Their criminal pasts, if they have one, and behavior leading up to the violence, examined and analyzed as if justifications can be found for the inhumane treatment—painfully reminiscent of discussions of what a female rape victim was wearing and doing before the violence against her occurred.

Repeatedly a "blame game" effect occurs that attempts to shift culpability from the perpetrator to the victim. Rationales that attempt to excuse what would otherwise be recognized as inherent biases are splashed across television screens in reports following up on these modern day lynchings. And typically in these cases the magnifying glass and/or the blame moves from law enforcement agents to the Black males who have been killed, affecting the decision to press charges or in the jury's ultimate ruling.

Dr. Kimberle Crenshaw, co-founder of the African American Policy Forum (AAPF), reminds us that Black women too are victims of similar state-sponsored violence, and that the perpetrators (individuals and systems) of their deaths are equally not held accountable. AAPF's "Say Her Name" campaign has brought visibility to those women who have been killed by the police but have been ignored by the media and forgotten by the public. The campaign aims to "shed light on Black women's experiences of police violence in an effort to support a gender inclusive approach to racial justice that centers all Black lives equally."

Dr. David Williams, an esteemed African American social science scholar, defines racism as "an organized system, premised on the categorization and ranking of social groups into races, and devalues, disempowers and differentially allocates desirable societal opportunities and resources to racial groups regarded as inferior." Everyone in such a parasitic structure participates, and everyone is impacted. Those who belong to the supremacist group benefit and gain privilege whether they partake actively or passively, and as such are debased by racism; those in the disempowered groups are disadvantaged in their access to resources and power, and always have to fight for their humanity. Racism creates a demotivating drive for change for those in power and an ineffective one for those without. Over 100 years post-slavery, Black people continue to struggle for power, wealth, and health, and remain at the bottom of the heap for all health indicators, weathering overt and micro aggressions against themselves and their communities.

As much as we point out at many of the injustices we suffer from, we must also point inwards and acknowledge that we must be instrumental in our own healing and salvation. Absolutely things have to change in broader society for anything we do to be effective and sustainable; however, without us being a catalyst the status quo will hum happily along as it currently exists. In the history of humankind, power has never voluntarily disaggregated itself, and those who are oppressed have always had to fight for their freedom. We must add our modern day fight to the many historic instances throughout the Black diaspora when we valiantly resisted bondage and subhuman insubordination in the face of relentless intimidation, losses, defeats, and death.

Too many of these acts of rebellion are frequently unacknowledged and not given the rightful place in our shared history. Such fearless acts began with jumping off slave ships into the deep unknown waters. Those who did not or could not take the leap continued their bravery over the centuries and generations with acts such as the creation of freed maroon colonies in the mountains; slave uprisings and rebellions; migration to less hostile diaspora environments; return to the homeland; spiritual levitations; armed and non-violent protests to gain legislated justice; marches and online acts of disobedience and disruptions.

To counter the resistance, white supremacy has historically tried to declare those who protest, resist, and refuse to succumb as either insane or criminal. During slavery, those who tried to escape captivity were considered to have a mental illness "draeptomania," the cure for which was "whipping the devil out of us." In the book *Protest Psychosis*, Dr. John Metzl documents how the diagnosis of schizophrenia—which had previously been portrayed in the 1920s as a pastoral illness of white suburban women—shifted in the 1960s to portray Black men of the civil rights era as angry, aggressive, criminal (e.g. the Black Panthers, a resistance group whose original name was fittingly The Black Panther Party for Self Defense), or criminally insane. These were the markers put on the Black Panthers by the system to validate unlawfully monitoring and arresting members in order to undermine and disrupt their protest.

More recently, the Black Lives Matter Movement (BLM), which began as a hashtag protest movement to peaceably disrupt and dismantle anti-Black policies, has now been branded a terrorist organization whose existence denies that all lives matter. Professional football players taking a knee during the national anthem to symbolically and non-aggressively voice their concerns over police brutality have been labeled unpatriotic and accused of desecrating the country's flag. This is not a coincidence. It is a pattern. The way Martin Luther King is currently deified by majorities in the country, even many Blacks would be stunned to learn that, in his time MLK, was considered an instigator of violence against white people; it was thought he asked for too much too soon. He too, like our Black football players, was told it wasn't the right time/way/reason to protest.

Regardless of these examples of backlash and resistance we have faced to our fight, continuing to write a journey of rebellion is imperative to our healing and healthy survival. We must dismantle the myth that there is a hierarchy of human value and begin to create a society where all individuals have similar chances to prosper without either hindrance or privilege. Multiple synergistic forces must work collectively and strategically to deconstruct and disrupt the caste system of racism, as we simultaneously imagine and reconstruct a more equitable society. The Black Lives Matter manifesto, one that seeks to disrupt anti-Black policies and practices, is one such bold example of concrete pathways that can begin to undo structural racism.

At the same time, but equally as important, is our overdue work on the individual level. A group can only be healthy if the individuals who make up the group are healthy. Each member of the Black community must find their healing pathway to minimize the damage of the trauma of racism—current, historical, and intergenerational. As individuals within the collective move toward being healthy, it's easier for those who are not as healthy or motivated to move forward when they see models of healthy activity around them. We have now witnessed the risk of allowing the seeds of racism to regenerate underground. The time is upon us to do the work to heal in order to improve our individual chance of survival as we repair and revitalize our communities in a way that will sincerely shed the chains of slavery and move us to legitimate levels of equality and power in our country.

Black While...

If you're reading this book, you likely do not need to be reminded what micro aggressions look like and feel like in the day to day world of Black people. But if there is any hesitation around the currency of these happenings, any pushback that maybe they are not as pervasive in our lives as in the past, the following collection of recent stories provide a tiny sampling of examples of the compounding harassment and stressful interactions that occurred far too easily and frequently in our lives in 2018.

Paul Butler, a Georgetown law professor and author of *Chokehold: Policing Black Men*, said encounters of police being called on Black people go back long before Harvard professor Henry Louis Gates, Jr. was arrested by police on his own front porch in 2009 after a neighbor mistakenly reported he was trespassing. At that time President Barack Obama had a "Beer Summit" with the esteemed professor and the arresting officer. He, like many of us, hoped it would be as he called it: "a teachable moment."

The lesson didn't take. Instead, beginning with the first instance noted below that happened at a Starbucks coffee shop, people have taken to social media to document and raise awareness of these types of injuries inflicted on Black people daily. They are notable not only because our benign actions are misinterpreted, stereotyped, and singled out, but also because it forces us into exchanges with the police despite our painful history of so many of them going wrong. Deadly wrong. It's a poignant reminder of how hard it is, even in 2018, to be Black while…

…Waiting in a Starbucks. On April 10, two Black realtors unintentionally began this wave of national awareness when they were arrested for trespassing and removed from a Philadelphia Starbucks by police officers. "Creating an environment that is both safe and welcoming for everyone is paramount for every store," Starbucks CEO Kevin Johnson apologized for the "misunderstanding." But his store manager had apparently not read the company handbook. She was so offended that the men had not purchased anything before asking to use the restroom that, despite this being completely acceptable per Starbucks policy, she called the cops. The men had been waiting for a third party to join them for a meeting…only he arrived to see them in handcuffs.

…Opening your own store. In San Francisco on July 17, Gourmonade owner Vicktor Stevenson was ironically on the phone with the security company of his business when four police officers showed up due to a report of someone breaking into a store. Initially, Stevenson, who also works at a Barbershop and was working hard to get his lemonade business up and afloat, thought he'd set off his security alarm by accident. He thought they were responding to assist him, only to be corrected and told that calls had actually been made pointing fingers at him. Thankfully Stevenson was able to show he owned the business without incident by unlocking the doors and providing ID.

…Mourning. White Catholic priest Michael Briese halted a June 27 funeral service in Charlotte Hall, Maryland and had a Black family and their deceased relative removed from the church. Why? Because an attendee of the funeral accidentally knocked over a chalice while trying to hug someone. "There will be no funeral, no repast, everyone get the hell out of my church," were the words the spiritual leader told the stunned, grieving family. Briese could not summon the spirit of forgiveness over the accident necessary to allow Ms. Hicks to be laid to rest in the church she was baptized and to accommodate her already anguished family.

…Running for public office. On July 3, Black Oregon State Representative Janelle Bynum's Facebook update was that someone called the police on her while she was canvassing door-to-door in her district. Bynum represents District 51, which includes the area of Clackamas County, where she was campaigning. A woman notified police and explained that Bynum was suspicious because she was "spending a lot of time typing on my cell phone after each house."

…Mowing the lawn. A 12-year-old rising 7th grader started a lawn mowing business when he got bored. Reggie Fields runs Mr. Reggie's Lawn Cutting Service in the Cleveland, OH suburb of Maple Heights. Most are impressed by and supportive of this type of adolescent activity. But not the neighbors he came across during the last week of June. They saw no value in his entrepreneurial spirit, decided against going out to speak to either him or his client, and instead called the police when he and his crew of siblings and cousins accidentally mowed a strip of lawn on their property.

…Barbecuing. In Merritt Park in Oakland, CA on April 29, Jennifer Schulte was quick to grab her phone to protect the community from Onsayo Abram. In Schulte's eyes, Abram and his family committed the crime of using a non-charcoal grill in the charcoal grill designated barbecue area. Snider was correct that they were using the wrong type of equipment, but rather than ignoring the harmless error or contacting park officials, Schulte felt emergency first responders were a better use of public resources.

…Selling water. Having a neighborhood stand is a right of passage for lots of kids. Many fall back on lemonade, but others are more original and will sell cookies, brownies, and so much more. On June 23, Alison Ettel did not give 8-year-old Jordan Rodgers any support or praise for choosing to sell healthy bottled water in her effort to raise money to go to Disneyland. Instead, she attempted to call the cops to shut down Rodgers' fairytale dreams.

…Playing golf. No matter that golf is called a "gentleman's game," there was no civility offered to five Black women on April 21, when the women were told by owners and employees of the Grandview Golf Course in York County, PA that they were taking too long. In what was their first time on the Grandview course as members, the women felt rusty but not that they were affecting any one else's game. One of the men playing behind them said their speed "did not slow his group down in any way." Nonetheless, the club management called 911 to have the four women removed from the course and offered to refund the women's memberships.

…Swimming in a pool. Skin-care consultant Stephanie Sebby-Strempel had a momentous day on June 24 in Summerville, SC. She hit a 15-year-old Black teen in the face and chest in an effort to get him to leave the pool because she felt he did not belong there. She was charged with assault on the teen, resisting arrest for biting one arresting officer and pushing another, and ultimately fired from her freelance job. She was not charged for calling the teen the N-word and trying to evict him from the community pool, though a family friend who lives in the neighborhood had invited him there.

…Inspecting investment property. In Memphis, TN on May 5, 2018, real estate investor Michael Hayes says that despite the fact that he showed her his investment contract and a statement from the owner that he had permission to enter the home, a white neighbor still called the cops on him and reported him trespassing. Fortunately, the level-headed officers intervened on his behalf when the unidentified neighbor stated she had friends in the sheriff's office. "I don't care if you're friends with the president," one of the policemen told her. "You're going to let him do what he's going to do." Still, concerned for his personal safety, Hayes asked and the officers remained while he took his final pictures.

…Leaving an Airbnb. Kells Fyffe-Marshall recalled her shock on April 30 when the police were called on her and two other Black filmmakers as they loaded their car to leave an Airbnb rental. Apparently, a white neighbor was aggrieved when she waved at them and they didn't respond, immediately moving her to report criminal suspicion. The group did not realize anything was amiss until 20 minutes later when they were tracked by helicopter and car patrol units as they went on their way. It took 45 minutes, their booking confirmations, and a call to their Airbnb host before the officers believed they had not been stealing items and had them packed in their suitcases, but had simply left a rental.

…Buying cellphones. Dorian Johnson and his uncle Vincent Lemar stopped by a T-Mobile in Fresno, CA on June 25 to look into buying new phones. That was their first mistake. Their second, most important, error was being Black. Despite the fact that Dorian Johnson was wearing the ID badge around his neck of the job he was going to once he left the store, he still looked criminal to store employees. They called 911 to report a burglary. Johnson and Lemar were forced to crawl from the store on the ground towards the police who had guns drawn on them, they were handcuffed and "verified" before anyone would believe these men simply wanted to upgrade their cellphones.

…Taking a nap. Black Yale graduate student Lolade

Siyonbola got a very tough lesson when, during an all-nighter of writing papers, she took a nap in the common room of the dorm she lives in on the university campus. Despite paying her tuition like everyone else, Siyonbola said a white female student flipped on the lights of the common room, told her she had no right to sleep there, and then called the police to report "an unauthorized person in the common room." Siyonbola had to unlock her dorm room door and hand over her ID before she was left alone to continue her attempt to simply get some rest and finish her schoolwork.

…Being a fireman. It wasn't Black firefighter Kevin Moore who wrote the Facebook post about his unfair treatment, but his fellow firefighter Megan Bryan. Bryan was completely livid at the racism shown to Moore as they completed annual routine inspections in upscale Oakland Hills in the Bay Area. Like the other firefighters, Moore wore his city issued uniform while he performed the inspections and carried a radio and clipboard. Still, one resident called the fire department to confirm that they were actually performing inspections and sent security footage of Moore to the police department because she "suspected 'criminal activity' at her house". Another neighbor approached him while video recording him on a phone and demanded his ID. Bryan said neither she nor any of their other crewmembers had ever been reported or asked for ID.

…Depositing a state-issued check. The police weren't called in this instance, but it gets a special mention because of the stinging irony of a double-dose of the system walking all over the back of an exonerated Black man named Darryl Fulton. Gainfully employed in a factory since his release, Fulton tried to deposit the state's restitution check for wrongfully incarcerating him for 23 years. In July 2018 a Chase branch in Franklin Park, Chicago, for no reason they ultimately could defend, twice refused to deposit his state-issued check. Ultimately, his lawyer stepped in and responded to the bank's apology that he would take his $169,876 check elsewhere.

…Walking. Sometimes the police show up without being called by a "Permit Patty" or "BBQ Betsy" as some of the people instigating calls to the cops have been dubbed in social media. In 2017 the American Civil Liberties Union of Wisconsin knew there was an institutional-level problem pre-dating the Starbucks incident. The ACLU sued the Milwaukee police department after finding that Milwaukee police officers made more than 350,000 traffic and pedestrian stops from 2010 to 2017 for which they have no record explaining probable cause for the interaction. The rate at which Black residents were detained in these traffic or pedestrian stops was more than six times higher than whites.

Chapter 2

Nature Or Nurture?

Over the life course, the energy needed to continually resist and struggle to exist in one's wholeness is exhausting. But longitudinal studies—a research method in which data is gathered on the same subjects repeatedly over a period of time—have shown much more than weariness has been burdening Black people and their communities. This type of research has established that if individuals are repeatedly forced to adapt to psychosocial stressors and adverse environments, the cumulative negative impacts eventually deregulate our body's attempt to regain equilibrium. In this way, white supremacy's insidious existence in the societal, political, and economic structures in which we have lived for centuries has been a compounding negative force. The result of this traumatizing terrorism of white supremacy has been the disruption and damage of all aspects of Black people's health—mental and physical.

Neuroscientists Peter Sterling and Joseph Eyer introduced the theory of allostasis to explain the physiological basis for disparate patterns of morbidity and mortality, especially amongst African Americans. Allostasis is the process by which our bodies adapt to stressful situations by creating "stability through change" and recalibrating homeostatic parameters to meet environmental demands. The brain perceives what is threatening and determines how we will respond to stressors. During the allostatic process, when our brain perceives a threat to the integrity of our body and/or mind, certain cells are recruited and galvanized to create stability, in order to support the systems that are essential to life.

Adrenal "stress" hormones, neurotransmitters, or immuno-cytokines are the substances that facilitate allostasis. But, if these mediators are released too often or are insufficiently managed by our bodies, there is cumulative wear and tear on the body called "allostatic load." Eventually the exposure to prolonged and excessive psychosocial and environmental stressors creates so much wear and tear on the body that it results in an inevitable loss of our body's adaptive plasticity and resilience.

Sterling and Eyer's work in this field came from observing and delving into real life examples of this, which helped to push the field into further exploration:

> For several decades, I combined research and teaching in neuroscience with social activism. In the mid-1960's, canvassing door-to-door in African American ghettos such as Central and Hough in Cleveland, I noticed that many people who answered my knock were partially paralyzed— faces sagging on one side, walking with a limp and a crutch. The cause was stroke, a rare affliction in my own community, and one that I never encountered later when canvassing in white, upper class Brookline. What caused so many strokes, I wondered, and how might they be connected to Cleveland's racial segregation? Arriving around 1970 at the University of Pennsylvania, I found that Joseph Eyer, another biologist/activist, had assembled clear epidemiologic evidence that stroke and heart disease, and their precursor, hypertension, all accompany various forms of social disruption, including migration, industrialization, urbanization, segregation, unemployment

and divorce.

Sterling and Eyer are not the only ones to begin seeing the connections. In calculations of allostatic load scores, behavioral scientist Arline T. Geronimus found that Blacks scored higher than whites, but that the differences could not be explained by poverty alone. When she looked at the primary mediators of allostasis, it became clear to her that the high levels of susceptibility and prevalence in Black communities were not as easily written off as simply African American genetics. As our bodies struggle to maintain stability, surpluses of stress hormones, neurotransmitters, and immune cytokines are released. This excessive activation leads to the stress-related disorders found in high levels in Black communities, such as anxiety disorders, depression, metabolic syndromes, cardiac diseases, infection, and violence.

When environmental factors are brought into the equation, it becomes clear that it is not natural inevitability or coincidence that research has repeatedly shown associations between racial discrimination and cardiovascular diseases, low-birth weight, poor sleep, mood disorders, and increased mortality. Geronimus applied the theory of allostatic load and developed the "weathering" framework to demonstrate the particular burdens of racial inequality on women's health regardless of socioeconomic status. She concluded that weathering is "a consequence of the cumulative impact of repeated experience with social, economic, or political exclusion." Weathering explains the particular burdens of racial inequity on Black women's reproductive health—deterioration in reproductive health status over the childbearing years, which leads to disparities in infant mortality and low birth weight babies. Such poor health outcomes are not attributable to unhealthy choices alone.

Rather, weathering is due to socio-economic cumulative disadvantage, in particular the duration of exposure to low-income, under-resourced communities.

Allostatic loading has contributed to our understanding of the new science of epigenetics, which has shed eye-opening attention on psychological and physiological patterns in our communities, some of which were, at times, falsely explained as caused by genetics. Epigenetics studies the relationship between the environment (stress, pollutants, nutrition, behavior), genes, and health. Epigenetics explain our ability to adapt and our compensatory genomic and neural plasticity that arise in response to facing unreliable and hostile environments. Epigenetics can be thought of as explaining how the environment, nurturing or not, can change the nature of our biology. It also provides a credible theory for non-genetic disease transmission.

Neuroendocrinologist Dr. Bruce McEwen explains that allostasis and allostatic loads epigenetically affect our "neural and systemic processes over the life course." These epigenetic changes occur through modifications in our cells that impact our gene expression, but they do not change the structure of the genes themselves. Epigenetic changes impact the activity of DNA segments—such as how the gene is expressed and produces protein or whether the gene is made into its gene products or not—without changing fundamentals of the DNA sequence we were born with.

Behavioral epigenetics research shows that present traumas or the traumas our ancestors experienced can also influence how our genes get expressed. As allostatic hormonal changes allow the brain to adapt in response to stressful stimuli, the resultant changes in our brain also feed back to the brain epigenetically. According to neurobiologist and trauma expert Dr. Rachel Yehuda, these epigenetic changes occur to increase our repertoire of possible survival responses to the overwhelming stressors. Depending on the situation, external traumas may cause genes to become dormant or to become more active, depending on which is most suitable for survival. However, such responses can create harm and diseases in someone who is continuously primed to stress even when they are in an environment without these stressors and no longer need to have this biologic predisposition to be hyper-aroused. When a person is primed to stress their body's learned behavior causes them to respond with paranoia, which can lead to withdrawal or aggression.

As descendants of the African slave trade, allostatic loading and the resultant epigenetic modifications explain how oppression has 'gotten under our skin' and to this day continues to impact our physical and mental health. There is now ample evidence to show that children born to mothers with Post Traumatic Stress Disorder (PTSD) are much more vulnerable to developing PTSD. Dr. Yehuda's research reveals that some of these changes occur in-utero and can impact "developmental programming" as well as how the infant responds to stress along their developmental trajectory. There is also evidence that patients suffering from depression show higher epigenetic aging, especially if they have a history of childhood trauma.

As promising as these scientific advances are in exploring alternate causes of the prevalence of stress-related diseases and high rates of violent activities in our communities, we must always be cautious when genetics is introduced into explanations about race and biology. Past and recent eugenicists and reformers have used biologic hereditary claims to deem inferior, enslave, and eradicate Black and non-Aryan people. As was stated by legal scholar and activist Dorothy Roberts, "It is when scientists and doctors insist that their use of race is purely biological that we should be most wary." While this theory shows us how much individual and communal areas have the potential for healing, we must be vigilant of attempts to twistedly use this science to further our existing oppression.

On the psychological level, one of the most insidious, pernicious, and oftentimes overlooked side effects that can result from the long term bombardment of the external trauma of racist norms and messages is internalized self-hatred. Positioning whiteness at the top and relegating Blackness to the bottom is toxic to our individual and collective self-esteem and self-worth. Sixty years ago, Martinique born psychiatrist Frantz Fanon argued that in the unconscious cultural archetype, Black people too have internalized Blackness as the lowest value, and have internalized all the negatives and prejudices that have been told about us/projected onto us by Europeans. In other words, we too are victims of "negrophobia," with the Negro symbolizing sin, the lower emotions, the baser inclinations, and the dark side of the soul. Unconsciously, we have come to distrust what is "black in me."

> Blackness, darkness, shadow, shades, night, the labyrinths of the earth, abysmal depths, blackens someone's reputation; and, on the other side, the bright look of innocence, the white dove of peace, magical, heavenly light. A magnificent blond child—how much peace there is in that phrase, how much joy, and above all how much hope! There is no comparison with a magnificent Black child: literally, such a thing is unwonted.

In many instances, having to deal with the inferiorizing stare of whiteness that ends on the surface of our skin causes us to "split off" how we are seen/experienced by whiteness. We take a second to determine which part of our Self will show out, and we respond depending on the degree of safety we calculate in the situation. Is it the angry Self, the seductive Self, the "mammie" Self, or will it be who we truly who are—no masks allowed? Over time and generations, we lose the continuity of Self. This practiced self-state switch leaves its scars, diminishes our ability to operate from a cohesive sense of self, and make us all the more vulnerable to the development of dissociative disorders like PTSD and depression.

Archbishop Desmond Tutu in a 2014 interview described when he became aware of his own internalized self-hatred. He got on a plane from Lagos, Nigeria and noticed he had two Black pilots flying the plane. At first he said, "I just grew inches; it was fantastic; because we were told that Blacks can't do this." The takeoff was smooth, but they soon hit turbulence. He recalled not believing that his first subconscious thought was, "Hey, there is no white man in the cockpit. Are those Blacks going to be able to make it?"

Until that point he realized that he had not known how "damaged" he was; what white people had drummed into their heads in South Africa about Blacks being inferior and incapable had been lodged somewhere in his head. "We are damaged, wounded people," he concluded. The slain apartheid freedom fighter Steve Biko captured this sentiment when he stated, "the most potent weapon in the hand of the oppressor is the mind of the oppressed."

Similar to Biko, psychiatrists William H. Grier and Price M. Cobbs, in their seminal book *Black Rage*, declared that Black people are "at one end of a psychological continuum which reaches back in time to his enslaved ancestors." It is as if our existence is never fully free to exist only in the present; there is always an ugly past that we have to confront.

Acclaimed researcher and educator Dr. Joy DeGruy Leary labeled this reactive traumatic psychological continuum in Black people as "post-traumatic slave syndrome." She argued that many of us are suffering from the multigenerational transmission of trauma that began during slavery and continues with present day oppression and institutionalized racism:

> One hundred and eighty years of the Middle Passage, 246 years of slavery, rape and abuse; one hundred years of illusory freedom. Black codes, convict leasing, Jim Crow, all codified by our national institutions. Lynching, medical experimentation, disenfranchisement, redlining, grossly unequal treatment in almost every aspect of our society, brutality at the hands of those charged with protecting and serving. Being undesirable strangers in the only land we know...Three Hundred and eighty-five years of physical, psychological and spiritual torture has left their mark.

Fortunately, epigenetic studies also show the potential for genetic changes caused by environmental exposures to be reversed and give expanded options for healing responses. Allostasis and epigenetics demonstrate the plasticity and resilience of the body as it attempts to adapt to its environments and optimize our options for response. Unless the body is stressed beyond its "yield point," meaning that its systems are deformed beyond their capacity to return to their usual functioning—making the deformation permanent and irreversible—the body is capable of repair and creating a new equilibrium.

Integrative medicinal approaches offer much hope for reversing the pathology of allostatic loading that result in pathologic epigenetic changes. Integrative medicine adopts a holistic mind/body/sprit or "whole body" approach and attempts to identify the functional pathways that govern healing. This is different from traditional western medical approaches in which symptoms are isolated and treatment is targeted to cells and diseased organ systems without consideration for the relationship of all body systems and our relationship to the universe at large. Integrative medicinal healing is thought to occur in part due to epigenetic mechanisms that tap into the natural wisdom of the body. This is particularly true when applied to lifestyle illnesses such as obesity, cancer, diabetes, and cardiovascular diseases that disproportionately impact Black people and are thought to result from improper nutrition, exercise, and environmental exposures and stress.

A recent scientific review article by scientists from Howard University, the University of California, and the Chopra Foundation hypothesized that integrative medicine impacts healing through the environment-body and mind-body interface through epigenetic pathways. They argue that parameters such as diet and exercise represent prominent elements in the induction of epigenetic changes and can result in health benefits through regulating the genes. They note that nutritional compounds and phytochemicals (plant-based) are the most potent regulators of epigenetic function, but that this modulation can be reversible and/or heritable.

The good news is that many of the complementary healing practices that are part of integrative medicine have existed in many traditional/indigenous healing sciences. Examples are: 1) use of natural products such as herbs, vitamins, and supplements; 2) mind-body practices such as yoga, tai chi, qi gong, pilates, deep breathing and relaxation exercises, acupuncture, meditation, massage, and aromatherapy; and 3) other health approaches such as Ayurvedic medicine, homeopathy, naturopathy, and traditional Chinese medicine. For example, the underlying philosophy in traditional

Chinese medicine is that the human body exists in organic unity with the universe, and balancing and harmonizing the inner Self with the outer world achieves health. Many of these practices force us to integrate the knowing of our mind with the feeling of our body.

Of note: psychotherapy, the mainstay of most mental health practices and about which I will elaborate later, has been found to induce positive epigenetic changes in the brain and is capable of healing trauma-related disorders. Clearly our inherited biology does not always have to be our destiny and we might be able to reverse some of the negative conditioning that oppression has burdened us with. We can't change the past, but we can imagine and create a brighter future. Indeed, being victims of oppression, we are perhaps best positioned to work to end oppression in all shapes and forms—race, gender, sexual, and class.

CHAPTER 3

Injurious Cultural Experiences

According to the Merriam Webster dictionary, culture is the way of life of a particular people as shown in their ordinary behaviors and habits, their attitudes toward each other, and their moral and religious beliefs, customs, and art. Culture reflects the sum total of a group of people bound together by a common history, place, and/or time.

Even though people of the African diaspora live in different geographies across the world, the shared history of enslavement and continued racial oppression create similarities across the globe, as seen in our art, our movement, our dance, our music, and our food. In many of these diasporic places, our quest for liberation and for respect for our full humanity unites us. The good news is that our current existence is evidence that, in spite of it all, Black diaspora culture has been very resilient and dynamic in the midst of our endangerment from white supremacy and has significantly curtailed their quest for our total annihilation.

But there is a cost that we have had to pay in our struggle to survive. The major function of culture is to be adaptive and dynamic, to create cultural belief systems and practices that adjust to changing environments so as to promote our survival and beyond. However, within the ever-existing systems of oppression, some aspects of Black culture are being pushed closer and closer to the "yield-point."

Some aspects of our culture now appear to have been stretched beyond plasticity and into stagnation. I have coined the term "culturostatic loading" to reflect this collective summation of allostatic overload that has been observed in Black people. Culturostatic loading describes the wear and tear on Black culture that has come from our collective traumas, and the destruction of some of our socio-cultural norms and beliefs. The loss of plasticity mentioned before has taken root and our culture rendered only marginally capable of resisting, bouncing back, and finding a new, healthier equilibrium.

For example, in spite of disparately high rates of obesity and the resultant cardiovascular effects in Black people—diabetes and hypertension—Black food norms continue to reflect the unhealthy patterns forced upon us during slavery. This is occurring in an environment where green, farm to table, vegan, and organic are the buzzwords for high sales in food for other communities. Survival during slavery days meant eating that which was discarded from the tables of whiteness, whose healthier vittles we had earlier prepared. Clearly, we have been ripped from healthier African ancestral cultural norms that minimized fast-cooked, animal-based foods and instead utilized farm-based, plant-based, and slower-cooked foods.

This critique does not ignore the reality of how poverty in poor Black neighborhoods has created an abundance of corner stores and fast-food joints with little or no access to healthy foods and fitness/recreational options. However, the reality that we all must face, rich, poor or in between, is that if we let go of our body, it will slowly let go of us. With each bite of processed, sugar, and fat laden foods we are slowly kissing our selves "goodbye." In the meantime, those of us with the agency to advocate for undoing these self-defeating "conveniences" and eradicate poverty, our personal responsibility is to find ways to balance our essential internal body needs with non-essential external needs. We have to balance pleasure with reality principles. Eat to live versus the other way around, living to eat.

As was stated earlier, in order to be life preserving and enhancing for any given group, culture has to be dynamic, constantly shaping and remaking itself. It is therefore doubtful and unlikely that the Black collective is consciously accepting its slow killer, morbid obesity, as a new cultural norm. Black culture might simply need a spark of remembrance of our grandmothers' vegetable gardens, or the ways in which one pig or goat had to be stretched to serve a whole village, or the ways in which Mondays, the wash day, was rice and red beans day, to reset and ignite new possibilities of healthier foods.

Another example is that of our cultural response to the HIV epidemic, one that disproportionately impacts the African American population. Black culture has lagged behind in creating new cultural norms to eradicate gender inequities and homophobia, key contributors to the amplification of the epidemic. Misplaced religious bigotry and zealotry has resulted in poisonous social stigma, forcing many same gender loving Black people to struggle to truly accept their full humanity and right to love whom they love. Many struggle with mental disorders and even death as a result of being pushed away from their families and communities. And as we have pushed many same gender loving people into the closet, some have lived in secrecy, fearful of honesty and full disclosure in their intimate partner relationships, which at times has endangered the health of their partners.

I conducted psychotherapy with a thirty-five-year-old African American, HIV positive male who was addicted to crack cocaine.

Therapy revealed his inability to accept and integrate his homosexual attraction and behaviors into his conscious construct of who he was, i.e. his identity. His homosexual-behaving identity was compartmentalized and not accessible to his conscious Self. He rationalized these behaviors as foreign to himself and occurring only while he was on base and altered by a few drinks.

With such fragmentation of his Self, he could not internalize HIV prevention messages as being directed at him and did not heed the life-saving education. In his everyday life, his identity was being strictly heterosexual and married—no need to wear condoms with his wife. And, he could not consciously engage in safe sex with male partners, for that would be admitting and owning his same-sex attractions and behaviors. As a result, not only was he dying of AIDS when he came to therapy, he had also infected his wife. He was extremely angry with her for divorcing him; in his eyes, he had done nothing to deserve her abandonment. He could not accept his fatal status, much less the one he inflicted upon her.

Again, it is highly unlikely that the Black collective unconscious is locked into lacking the ability to allow individuals to love whom they love. We should not accept that this is truly who we are, whom the divine life force and creator has anointed us to be—people who vilify and/or kill those who are have different gender and sexual identities. Many of these people are right next to us in the places where we worship, where we play, and where we work. Perhaps we should unblock our collective unconscious memory of pre-enslavement and pre-colonization spiritual practices, in which loving each tribal member fiercely and extending compassion to our enemies, even if they became our slaves, was our norm. Or maybe we could download authentic and compassionate Christian doctrine, which teaches us to love our neighbor as our Self.

Jamaica, my birthplace, has the reputation for being one of the most intolerant and homophobic countries in the world. One significant component of the violence that runs loose in the culture can be attributed to those who engage in same gender sexual relations; the need to destroy the evidence of that which shames them. This manifests in either taking his or her own life through suicide, or the life of the other person through homicide. I have been told of 106 of such deaths from the late 1980s to today. Surely we can do better than this!

Another cultural fallout is that of Black family-rearing customs normalizing male-absent households and romanticizing the single-unit strong Black female who struggles to be head of her family. Mass incarceration of Black males resulting from a pernicious criminal injustice system that escalated the war on drugs has impacted and destroyed Black life at multiple levels—the child without a father to protect them; the woman/man without a partner to share love and resources; the nephew without an uncle to guide; the neighborhood and community without a potential genius to lead its institutions. With the absence of fathers in many homes it's as if there were "male deserts" in many communities.

The majority of males I have worked with, especially when I worked in the prisons, either grew up without a male parent living in the home or one who was not psychologically present when physically there. The resultant psychological fallout from the physical or emotional absence of fathers in the lives of children is "father hunger." This is a condition wherein sons and daughters growing up without their father yearn, long for, and crave masculine energy. It is primarily unconscious, so oftentimes the child is not aware of how this emotional hunger is shaping their feelings, thoughts, and actions.

Father hunger is particularly damaging for males, who, without a replacement father figure, may grow up without consistent modeling of what it means to be "male" and how to construct a healthy masculine identity. Instead, they are left alone and without guidance to dream or fantasize of a father to love, correct, and protect them. For some, this can make them more vulnerable to negative social forces. Internalized negative media and blighted neighborhood stereotypes of Black manhood more easily take root in such vulnerable, hungry consciences.

My psychiatric practice has brought to me some very sad, painful examples of father hunger. Alvin was a 29-year-old electrician whom I saw in therapy shortly after his wife filed for divorce. He never knew his father. His mother was a sex worker and a substance abuser. He was left alone on many nights when his mother went out to work. She was physically abusive, necessitating his being hospitalized on several occasions. "She would beat me, then tell me she loved me."

Not surprisingly, his early school years were quite turbulent. He often got into fights, was truant, and underperformed academically. Fortunately, when he got to high school, a male teacher took special notice of him and served as a mentor; his academic performance as well as his behavior improved dramatically. Alvin joined the Air Force, where his hunger for male role models was significantly satiated, but upon discharge and the loss of these positive influences, his relationship with his high school sweetheart was not sufficient to supply him with the emotional support that he needed. He began using cocaine and alcohol, and his marriage quickly fell apart, as did he.

Philip was a 30-year-old engineer whom I saw in therapy after he was fired from his job for a positive drug screen. He had never met his biological father. Both his mother and stepfather were alcoholics and had a very violent relationship. During their many fights, he would often be sent away to family members. Both parents physically abused him, frequently stripping him naked and leaving him alone in the locked house after he was whipped. When he was five years old his stepfather began to sexually molest him; it did not end until he was eight years old. He started using drugs during adolescence. As he got older, most of his relationships were with prostitutes, many of whom he raped and battered. He divorced twice.

After observing this phenomenon of father hunger—present in a significant number of the youth that my non-profit public health organization the Institute for Women and Ethnic Studies (IWES) served in New Orleans public schools—I led a daylong convening of over 100 men from varied socioeconomic backgrounds to further delve into this issue. The purpose of the gathering was to explore how men in the community could better serve as mentors in young people's lives. The men were divided into small groups facilitated by other men and asked to reflect on their experiences of being fathered or serving as fathers in their children's lives. A very safe and warm environment was provided for them to internally explore and outwardly express.

Sadly, many expressed that this was the first time they experienced being heard and feeling that their voices mattered. And many came to their "aha moment" that the absence of fathers in their lives had not only been extremely painful while they were growing up, but had also created parenting patterns in their current lives that were unhealthy. Many shared their challenges with being a present father for their children, even if they lived in the home. And one young man, who was committed to do better with his children stated, "I saw my father after 20 years of his absence at the funeral of my brother. The streets claimed his life for was no father around to claim him. I miss my brother."

Father hunger also impacts girls/women. While their mothers may fill the need for role models, feelings of abandonment and not witnessing what good intimate relationships look like in their households can affect women's subsequent relationships and expectations of the men in their lives.

When I think of my father, there aren't many experiences to recount. My remembrance is his face peering into mine with a big grin on his face. But I'm somewhere between 9-11 years old in that memory. I don't remember if I ever saw my father before that. For a couple years after that he would show up in my world once or twice each year. We didn't do things like trips to ice cream stores or zoos or amusement parks; he mainly visited me at my grandmother's home where I was growing up. But they were happy experiences; he seemed so thrilled to spend time with me. I do remember that every time his parting words would be something along the line of, "your birthday is coming up! I'll see you then and I'll have something special for you." Or it would be Christmas coming…whichever was closer, he would promise to return bearing gifts.

I don't remember the exact point in that limited span of time that I learned as such a little girl that his promises were not the same as the promises of other adults in my life. He would not return as he said. He never ever showed up on my birthday. I never saw him or a present from him at Christmas. And the next time I would see him, he wouldn't even apologize for the broken promise made the last time.

Looking back, I'm sure he probably stopped thinking of

me the minute he walked out of the door and likely had no recollection of what he'd said the visit before. But I know no one had to tell me I could not depend on him. I remember smiling and nodding when he would utter his promise and then immediately locking it in the back of my mind when the door closed behind him. I guess I always learned quickly. It may have only been a couple times per year, but the pattern was still clear.

I never brought him up and the adults didn't really speak frequently of my father in my grandparents' household. But inevitably there were friends who, limited in the bubble of their nuclear family worlds, didn't understand why my father wasn't around and would poke at me for answers. I used to tell them that it didn't matter because my grandfather was like a father to me. I didn't need anything from my father so there was no reason for me to need him.

In hindsight, I'm not dismayed by the lie I told, but by the walls that I felt I had to learn so early in life to erect around my confused teenage heart. I didn't have any adults in my life I could talk to about it. I didn't want to show my friends I felt different and unwanted. And maybe it I believed it to some degree—it was true I didn't want for anything in terms of food, shelter and security. But I do know I quieted and locked away nagging thoughts that would pop into my head at times. I didn't understand why my father didn't show up. Why he would say that each time and disappear. Why he didn't love me like other fathers seemed to love their children. What was wrong with me?

As a progressive independent woman, in my twenties I

decided I would search for and reach out to my father. Of course, I was convinced that it wasn't because I felt I needed anything from him. Rather I felt it would be a boost to my own personal growth. I wanted to learn more about him and his side of my family that I knew of only through unreliable, second hand stories I would over hear protective elders in my family telling each other. When I tracked him down and got on the phone with him, we had a very stilted conversation. I told him I didn't want anything but to get to know him. His response, "I hope you won't be disappointed" put me off. I didn't follow up with him again.

I never told many people, but while what he said pissed me off, I was devastatingly struck by the voice on the phone that was a complete stranger to my ears. The voice that should be at the least familiar and at the most one of comfort and care sounded like any and everyone else. Other than his identifying himself, when he answered, there was nothing memorable in his voice for me to identify him from anyone else. There were neither good memories nor bad memories for it to evoke. No sense of history within the timbres of his voice. I was talking to a stranger.

That thought, that I didn't even know my own father's voice was more painful than his lack of awareness that he'd already disappointed me over a lifetime—that was the entirety of our relationship. And it was compounded by his self-image seeming his primary concern even as I approached him as someone who wanted nothing from him but conversation. It reinforced my feelings of being unattached and alone in the world with nothing that securely roots me to any part of it. My connections felt like loose strings to responsible adults who stepped in because they knew I had no one else to raise me in a reliable environment, not people who where in my life because of an innate parental instinct to be the one there for me. One half of the two people who should care about me unconditionally and more than anyone else, had not at all factored in my existence.

In my thirties I was attending a conference in the same town my father lived and to my surprise, he found out I was nearby and came to see me. We were able to carve out a couple hours before my flight left to return home and we had a conversation I will never forget. He shared a lot of stories about his and my mother's life around when I was born. He shared information about his siblings that answered unasked questions I had long had about why I was so different in so many ways from my mother's family. And just when I started to feel a sense of belonging and place in the world, and maybe even in his, he declared, "I've come to the point in my life when I no longer love my children. I like them. When you love someone, expectations are too high." I don't know what kind of satisfaction his copout from being vulnerable and taking emotional risks with his children gave him. But again, he reminded me that he would never be a safe place for me to land.

I should have long given up on believing there was a relationship of any kind worth paying attention to. I had admitted long ago that the insecurity I couldn't shake, the defensiveness I projected and the insufferable emotional pain I felt when I was vulnerable in my relationships made sense since from a child I'd felt alone and abandoned within my relationship with the man who gave life to me. I could hear myself over and over telling people in matter of fact terms about my relationship, or lack there of, with my father as if it was a simple story I was reciting, and not a deep haunting pain and hunger that I had in fact learned to live with and learned how to mask, but truly never got over. My father was like the one who got away. Despite my logical mind and voice understanding and naming how I'd moved on and away from the need for that relationship, in the recesses it could always be triggered that what if…

And triggered it was in my forties when I heard my father was seriously ill. Once more I reached out. Through my half-sister I found his current phone number and messaged him that I was concerned about him and his health. Despite a serious conflict of time and money with an important happening in my life, I began making space to go see him. But this time he didn't even put up the façade. He didn't respond but his phone app sent me confirmation that he had seen my message. Subsequently I saw him on social media tending to his relationship with those around him.

I'd like to say 100% truthfully that it didn't hurt me, that I felt no pain when he didn't respond. But I know that it's only because my walls are well erected and fortified. Had that father hunger not been there I wouldn't have even reached out after my hand had gotten scalded once too many times. I know deep down I was hoping for one of those deathbed reconciliations that make me bawl when I watch them in the movies. I wanted and yearned for that release of emotion that is more than finding out health history and personality types on his side of the family. I wanted to learn that I was wrong all these years; that I mattered deeply to him. That while a speck on the earth to everyone else, this man who is my father treasured my birth and my life. That it made a difference to him. That he loved me unconditionally from a far even if he'd never provided me food, shelter and security. But that was not the end to my drama with my father.

He's still alive and perhaps shortly when I venture into my fifties we may yet have another exchange in our every-decade pattern. I suspect I'm running out of time, but I'm using the interlude to understand what my lifetime dearth of affection from my father means for my current and next relationships, and sincerely trying not to worry about what ifs. It's crazy to think that a person who I've proba-bly been in front of or spoken to a total of maybe ten times in my 49 years of life could have such an over-whelming effect on my being. But he does. Largely detrimentally to date, my father is in every relationship I've had. Rather than thinking I'm so realized and self-developed that I am beyond this pain and hunger, I accept that it is a deep wound I work around every day. I just get better at doing so each decade.

Without a doubt, the Black child's development is heavily influenced by the dynamics with their caretakers, but it is ultimately a sum total of multiple interacting forces including the society at large, the community in which they are raised, and Black culture be it at the tribal, local, national, or global level. And, as set forth, these forces can be onerous.

Yet, in spite of all the oppressive barriers, losses and holes, Blackness and Black people have survived. One might argue that our existence is evidence of and a tribute to our ancestors' courage, resistance, and resilience–from the slave ships and cotton fields to the White House. Evidence that Black optimism, hope, and joy still prevail. But, there comes a point when the beaten up, punch-drunk prizefighter can no longer stand up and throw another punch. His/her legs are smashed and broken and he can no longer protect, hunt-gather for his family and community, or help shape the future for his child. On an individual and community level, our mission has to be curtailing the frequency of our culture taking shots in the boxing ring, reducing the stress on its plasticity, and restoring its beneficial function to us all.

Chapter 4

Injurious Childhood Experiences

Now that we have established the history and operation of this oppressive system that permeates many aspects of our lives and significantly damaged some of our cultural norms, it's important to take a look at the way it seeps into our household and can infect our community from infanthood. Sadly, sometimes indirectly and subconsciously, the disease of racism is transmitted via the ones we love the most. For many Black parents, their best efforts are already at a disadvantage due to the often unrealized dysfunction from their own childhood and complicated by the toxic stress of the racism they battle daily. Our continued existence, one in which some Black folks are thriving and striving, suggests that in spite of this continued oppressive bombardment, enough of our parents and families showed up for their infants with love and attunement.

And why is this important?

Infants are born helpless, unable to take care of their basic needs for nutrients, clothing, and shelter. As infants, our survival totally depends on the kindness, affectional bond, and unconditional love of our parent/caretaker. Without human touch in the first several days of our life, we would wither up and die. Not only must our basic need for food, clothing, and shelter be met, we need our caretaker to hold and comfort us, contain our anxieties, mirror our beauty, nudge us gently towards our potential, protect us, and correct us.

The quality of this nurturance and attachment to our caretaker lays the groundwork for our developing personality—that is, how we experience, perceive, and process our Self, others, and the world around us. The quality of attachment and attunement with our caretaker also lays the groundwork for how we will in turn take care of our Self throughout our lives. It is a relationship that is only successful as long as the participants who are in it are healthy. In order for an infant to feel secure in their attachment to their caretaker, the caretaker needs to be emotionally available, sensitive, and responsive.

Pediatrician and psychoanalyst D.W. Winnicott coined the term, "good enough mother." He argued that a mother's love and holding allows an infant to "come to feel that his body is himself and that his sense of self is centered in his body." It is this sense of self-connected continuity that will allow the child to consolidate a cohesive, non-dissociated identity at later developmental stages. Psychologist Erik Erickson built upon Winnicott's construct of the "good enough mother" in his theorizing of the notion of "good enough parenting" throughout the developmental stages.

Good enough parenting occurs when a caretaker meets most of their child's needs without undue hostility, aggression, excessiveness, and/or withholding, in order that a child might grow up with sufficient drive, basic virtue, and morality. Emotionally healthy caretakers are ones who are whole enough to suspend their narcissistic needs and perform good enough service to a helpless infant. For example, crying is an infant's primary communication of distress, be they hungry, soiled, frightened, or feeling unwell physically. The good enough caretaker will wake during the night and attend to the crying infant no matter how exhausted the caretaker is feeling. When an infant communicates distress and the caretaker soothes the infant, the loving nurturance creates a secure attachment that is essential for a child's mental well-being and resilience later in life.

Good enough parenting during infancy allows a child to exit from their inner cocoon and symbiotic relationship with their caretaker and venture into the outside world with enough trust and feeling of safety by the age of one-year-old. Otherwise, the child is at risk to view the world with mistrust and paranoia and will internalize and/or act out on those feelings.

Good enough parenting up to the age of three, which requires a continued healthy and affectional attachment to their caretaker, will propel the child into beginning the lifelong journey of autonomy, without undue feelings of shame or doubt. The child, when supported in being able to stand on their own feet, builds their confidence by being able to take on more independent activities without fear of being humiliated or shamed. The securely attached child will feel free to err, be silly, and/or to be ignorant. All the while, the good enough parent spares them from the possibilities of drifting into feelings of distress by not treating their trying-on behaviors as foolish. In other words, the child is spared "loss of face" i.e. self-esteem and not left with unnecessary worry about how others view them.

Between the ages of three to seven, good enough parenting is directed toward encouraging the child to take the initiative in exploring the external world with gusto while simultaneously indulging in their rich inner world of fantasy and imagination. By being allowed to take the initiative in making up and playing games and being praised for doing so, the child begins to develop a sense of purpose without feeling undue guilt for the pleasure they receive from their deepening mental powers. This, in combination with their increased locomotor ability, allows them to begin to value independence, which later in life helps them to manage their anxieties if/when they have to breech other people's limited expectations of their full capacities.

Between the ages of seven to eleven, good enough parenting in combination with teachers as parental extenders sets the stage for a child to learn the know-how of knowledge seeking and bringing forth their own wisdom. This helps them avoid the shame of feeling intellectually inferior and incompetent. It is during this period that a child begins to learn to regulate their impulses and need for immediate gratification, oftentimes abetted by internalizing their caretaker's moral code. As the child ages and increasingly interacts with the outer world, it is the history of loving attention to their empathic needs from childhood that supplies them with the necessary self-esteem to transition from the self-centeredness of infancy to the gradual development of the social skills needed to be cooperative and non-aggressive with others.

Good enough parenting during the teenage years supports a child's capacity to explore their multiple identities—sexual, racial, occupational, and philosophical. Good enough parenting allows the teenager to temporarily shift their primary attachment from parental figures as they seek out peers and other role models to try on new possibilities of Self. In the face of this seeming rejection, good enough parents do not withdraw. Instead, they continue to communicate to the teenager that they remain their secure and affectional center of attachment. This requires setting firm protective limits without an undue rigidity and punishments. Eventually, as the teenager transitions from childhood to adulthood with good enough parental, peer, and role model support during the turbulence, their identity will emerge with sufficient enough cohesion so that they can avoid feeling unstable and chaotic.

Over time, consistent good enough parenting, in addition to adequate social supports and relationships, help a child develop a baseline sense of Self as being whole, worthy, deserving, and lovable. This enables their transition into adulthood with enough efficacy, confidence, and resilience to successfully negotiate the multitude of challenges and obstacles that lay ahead. The now adult will be faced with the need to: develop the capacity for intimacy versus drifting into loneliness in young adulthood; be productive and creative in middle adulthood versus falling into stagnation and helpless inertia; and finally, be able in later years to adapt to the triumphs and disappointments that life has brought versus descending into despair and regretful hopelessness.

As psychiatrist Heinz Kohut stated, "But from the very beginning, this perfection of our self-esteem, this wish to exhibit and say, 'Look, whatever I am, I am,' is aided and abetted by the empathic mother's responsiveness." It may seem counter intuitive, but when a child is made to feel they are the center of the universe in the early years, it facilitates proper development of their self-worth and value. This early narcissism actually enables successful character development as the infant grows into a child and begins to separate from their caretaker and experience their own individuality. It shields the child appropriately as they are gradually exposed to and begin to accept the unavoidable, impending reality that they are just a small drop and a tiny speck in the vast universe. The grieving process that comes with the child's realization that they are separate from their caretaker, and their loss of omnipotence, is easier when they have earlier been made to feel that they matter and that they belong.

Good enough parenting, with its inherent secure attachment and affectional bond between child and caretaker, is key to the development of healthy personality styles in adulthood. Personality theorists such as Eve Caligor and Otto Kernberg postulate that an adult with a healthy personality experiences who they are as cohesive. They have a realistic sense of themselves and their significant other. They are able to pursue long-term goals and are satisfied by their commitments to work and relationships. In their relationships they display concern and empathy and are capable of true intimacy and vulnerability. They also use mature defenses that help them to adapt to conflicts without much distortion of reality, their moral compass and values are consistent and respectful of others, and during periods of intense emotionality they can maintain equanimity.

However, if a child's experience of being parented during childhood exposed them to non-nurturing, non-empathic, and adverse experiences, they are put at great risk during adulthood for developing poor physical and mental health, and worse, premature death. The Adverse Childhood Experiences (ACE) research study—conducted by physician Vincent Feliti in the 1980s with over 17,000 participants—found that sexual, physical and/or emotional abuse, emotional or physical neglect, and family dysfunction (such as growing up in a household where someone was an alcoholic, drug user, mentally ill, suicidal, where the mother was violently treated, or where a household member had been imprisoned) resulted in increased risk for mental and physical diseases. The study found that the higher the burden of adverse experiences during childhood, the higher the risk for engaging in risky behaviors such as smoking, substance use, multiple sex partners, early initiation of sex, and pregnancy. Eventually, the risk for dying early is greater, associated with mental, cardiovascular, pulmonary, and cardiovascular disease. An interesting finding was that a subset of the study participants who struggled with obesity were identified as having been sexually and/or physically abused as children.

Childhood maltreatment, as occurs with ACEs, contributes to over 30% of adult mental disorders. These environmental stressors in a child's life can influence the brain's stress response system and contribute to allostatic loading. The child's brain circuitry is forced to adapt to the stressors of hostile and unreliable parenting, and prepares the child for "fight or flight" in response to the danger and lack of protection for its survival. The changes and remodeling that the child's developing brain has to undergo to adapt and adjust can eventually create epigenetic changes that get expressed and can lead to later biologic and/or psychological dysfunction.

The following story demonstrates the interactive and multiplying impact of childhood adversity upon adult experiences:

My challenge has been that something happened to me when I was a child and no one paid any attention. My experiences were real, it happened, it shouldn't have, and that's because there was no adult protecting me and gently guiding me through the process.

In my 30s, I started asking myself—"What's wrong? What happened to me?" I came to realize that what was most prevalent in my life was FEAR–it had taken over my life–I spent more energy living with fear than working on women's hair. From the time I awakened to when I parked at the salon and started working on someone else, I was totally filled with fear. Once I started working I was okay; the salon was a safe space for me. And also for my clients. This is where they could let their hair be, or take off their wigs and be free of judgment. Hair says so much about where women are—that is where a lot of our stuff gets locked up.

When I moved to Seattle I realized that I had to restructure myself. I had to allow myself to play like a five-year-old because I missed all of that—my childhood. I have very little memory of being young. Someone once asked me if I remembered when we did something when I was thirteen years old, and I did not. All that comes up for me during that time is what happened to me at night. When the lights went out. And I kept it a secret as I was told that if I talked about what was happening, bad things would happen to me.

At some point the pain became so bad I had to take something to go to sleep and something to wake up. I ended up in a hospital. It was then I decided that I had to live differently. I was not afraid of therapy; I did that. I also added whole foods, walks in the park, and yoga. I also had to accept that I was beautiful. People used to always tell me that I was beautiful, but I didn't know how to deal with it. When I enrolled in a beauty school I started looking at beauty differently other than what had been going on back there in my head.

And another big thing I have had to overcome is SHAME. No one put it on me; I put it on myself. I was the one being ashamed of me. And I was only a child. I could not make the decision to rape me—so why was I ashamed?

With time I have come to realize that my caretaker did not know what she was doing to me—I can't hold her hostage now. When I heard her story now that we are older, I realized that back then she couldn't help me. She had so much love for this man, she could not see what he was doing, how he was manipulating and controlling her. For some women, if they are not being physically abused, they don't know they are being abused. Now she says, "I was stupid back then." They had so much shit going on, they did not think about me—if they ever did think about me. If you're keeping it moving, your child is being abused, or something else bad is happening to them—when you don't stop to think about what's happening, you are letting your child suffer. You're creating more of what you have.

Fear and shame are big. They take over. Most Black women hide behind it, dress it up, cover it over with expensive perms and weaves. Also with our religion, how can we call ourselves religious/spiritual if we are not working it out? I want ease, not to be in struggle. I back off from struggle. Many of the issues we face started before our parents, from way back in slavery. So why are we still choosing to live like we are still slaves? I won't make anyone make me a slave. I don't do anything I am not comfortable with.

As a child I was one of the biggest liars. It was my survival. This is why now as an adult, truth is so important to me. It's my serum. I catch myself when I am lying. I stop and tell the truth. I am not a victim of my past. I want to use my story to help other women.

It never goes away though. I can't undo what happened. But I am thankful for my experiences because they helped me see the truth. We can all choose—whether to stay victim or to be victorious.

When Self is not in harmony, the injured Self will most likely engage in injurious interpersonal experiences with others. This can manifest as mistrust, paranoia, and aggression directed at others as the injury within is externalized, sometimes onto those closest to us.

This is most problematic when these projections happen in relationship to raising our children—when we are not being good enough parents who suspend our narcissism so that we can love our children unconditionally and make them bask in that early, short-lived, protective infantile delusion that they are the center of the universe. Or, when we are not being emotionally and/or physically present enough to protect our children from sexual, physical, and emotional abuse.

I served as a psychotherapist in a Veterans Administration (VA) research project with over fifty crack-addicted African American males in the 1990s. These men were on their last legs, having experienced incarceration, loss of familial support, and homelessness. A common theme throughout all these cases was that none of the men felt deserving of being treated by a competent Black woman psychiatrist in a university setting. "Why would I waste my time with them," was a common inquiry. Deep inside, these men did to not feel that they were good enough, that they mattered to others, that they had a right to belong. It took several sessions before they could settle in, get present, and do the work. One of the first issues we always had to address was their history of being perpetrators in intimate partner violence, simultaneous with they themselves being childhood victims of either physical or sexual abuse.

Additionally, growing up Black and poor in Louisiana, a state with the one of the worst histories of slavery and current day mass incarceration, the men had never felt physically or psychologically safe in the larger community. Very little was expected of them, and they expected very little of themselves in return. As they approached early adulthood, they turned to cocaine, alcohol, and other drugs to avoid dealing with the harsh realities of their lives and to help soothe the pain of the compounding and overlapping societal and familial injuries they faced.

A decade later, I created an existential group psychotherapy program for older African American veterans who were dealing with PTSD and the moral injury they felt from having acted as "agents of killing," as many described themselves. Similar to the experience that I had earlier with other Black veterans, the men initially had difficulty accepting that I truly honored their humanity and wanted to facilitate an authentic healing process for them. It was an experience they seldom felt in the racist structures of the VA. Once the men began to trust my intentions and we were able to break that barrier down, many were pleasantly surprised to discover that they could work through vulnerabilities oftentimes related to their early childhood adversities, bring forth and create meaning for themselves, and share powerful philosophical ideals about the mystery of life.

The groups I've facilitated are glaring examples of how we pass injury down through generations as if it were in our DNA. When we become the objects that inflict adverse childhood experiences upon our Black children, we break the necessary pattern of good enough parenting discussed earlier and create the potential for a dysfunctional cycle to gain traction. It is difficult, however, to separate individual level pathology from the societal causation. For many Black parents, their dysfunctional child-rearing behaviors are not only a result of their own unresolved non-race related intrapsychic pain; their behaviors are compounded by the impact of the toxic stress of racism in their life. Racism injures our sense of Self and itself is a source of adverse childhood experiences for many.

CHAPTER 5

Injurious Societal Experiences

Ever since our forced exodus from the continent into captivity in the Western world—where we were stripped of our dignity and our unique cultural ways of being (religion, social order, language)— white supremacy has constantly denigrated our right to our full human existence and potential. What, therefore, does it mean to exist in the suffering placed upon Blackness as a woman or a man? We earlier explored how dysfunctional intra-familial interpersonal dynamics and injurious maladaptive cultural norms can harm our mental well-being and quality of life. We will now dig a bit deeper into how explicit external societal attitudes and beliefs regarding race and gender can wreak havoc on our being.

I spearheaded a project at the Institute of Women and Ethnic Studies in which we conducted Wisdom Circles with fifty-five African American women of varying socioeconomic status and age. This qualitative study was based on Dr. Melissa Harris-Perry's book, *Sister Citizen: Shame, Stereotypes, and Black Women in America*. The Wisdom Circles were to explore how stereotypes, shame, and racism shaped their self-esteem, self-efficacy, and agency. In her book, Harris-Perry hypothesizes that in their confrontation with race and gender stereotypes, African American women's citizenship is shaped by their attempts to navigate a room made crooked by stereotypes that have significant psychic consequences. The prevailing stereotypes include: Mammy, an asexual, loyal, and nurturing woman; Sapphire, a matriarchal and emasculating woman, also known as the strong Black woman; and Jezebel, an oversexed and over sexualized woman.

The overarching finding from this study affirmed that racism and sexism (or "racist patriarchy," as coined by Professor Kimberle Crenshaw) indeed made crooked every social, personal, and political room in these Black women's lives. As a result, for these women, chronic subconscious feelings of shame undermined self-esteem, relationships, and their confidence in their ability to fully pursue dreams, because many had internalized the negative stereotypes about themselves.

The most consuming and ever present theme that surfaced across all the stereotypes was the challenge Black women face in fully embracing their natural beauty—the Self we came into life with. Many recalled painful stories related to skin color and hair texture and had experienced difficulty internalizing a sense of beauty and glamor as it related to their own or others' negritude. The centuries of shaming about our physical appearance and the internalized notion that white people have superior looks seem to have decimated our ability to fully embrace the coarser texture of our hair (a hair that grows out, not down), our broader noses, our dark skin, and our thicker, fuller lips. A story shared with me highlights how readily this doubt can be planted in our heads, whether welcomed or not:

Before the days of the Kardashians anointing large lips acceptable and even aspirational, I remember being at the MAC cosmetics counter one day. A friendly and helpful white sales associate attended to me. She suggested a lip color to me and I told her I was hesitant to wear bright colors because I have large lips and I didn't want that single color to dominate my face. She replied, "that's not true, your lips aren't bad at all." She realized her own faux pas before I finished saying to her, "I said my lips were big, not that they were bad. I think my lips are one of my best features!" It was an uncomfortable moment for us both. I continued to let her help me, and I did buy a different product, but I've never forgotten how obviously the idea that "big lips = unattractive lips" was ingrained in her subconscious. Had I been at all unhappy about my lips it would have easily reinforced my negative feelings towards them. I hope we both learned something that day.

Not surprisingly, many of our Black men show a preference for white or light-skinned women as partners. This was very evident in more racially segregated (and more patriarchal) times, when the wives of many Black male professional lawyers, dentists, and doctors were almost all light-skinned. Currently, many wives/partners of Black athletes and entertainers are white or light skinned. These are all variations of the manifestation of an internalized negative construct of the Black Self.

Black men have not escaped this preferential value system regarding phenotypically white "Caucasoid" versus Black sub-Saharan "negroid" looks. This devaluation of Black beauty was played out on our television screens as we watched Michael Jackson alter his natural negroid looks year after year, becoming whiter and whiter in his appearance; and eventually fathering phenotypically appearing white children. It is stunning to consider what seems like a search for validation or acceptance plaguing someone so talented, successful, and universally celebrated. And while perhaps the most visible, he would be one of a long line of Black men who got their hair processed, "conked," and skin bleached.

Similar to race, gender is an equally damaging source of inferior-ization and powerlessness for Black women. The biblical construct of Eve as the source of evil paves the way for patriarchy to assert its dominance. The divine is almost always referred to in the masculine, depriving women of the ability to perceive constructs of the divine in their own feminine image, and in these religious constructs, women are blamed for being the source of many ills. Women are cast as being a castrating force upon men and held responsible for their shortcomings, their inability to control their sexual urges, and their resultant moral failures. This doctrine dictates the necessity for women to cover their sensuality, their hair, arms, and legs. Women are denied their pleasure zones as is seen in female genital mutilation. And some cultures decree that women lack sacredness when they bleed. During this natural cycle they are perceived as undesirable, unclean, and in need of segregation from men, their families, and God.

The gendered stereotype of Black women is deeply entrenched in and even promoted by our community. On a February 2015 episode of *The Nightly Show With Larry Wilmore*, five Black men defended the seemingly staggering statistics of single motherhood in the Black community and the assumption that this automatically correlates to a high level of absentee fathers. The men led a thoughtful discussion on how the data didn't account for their experience. They pointed out they had fathers who were not married to their mothers but still were very much present, stabilizing forces in their lives.

Their thoughtfulness about the damage of stereotypes in our community stopped at those concerning absentee fathers. And when they were asked as a fun final question, "Are there so many single Black women because Black women are too bossy?" and "On a scale from one to ten, are Black women too bossy?" The audience was greatly amused when all five men pretended to be so afraid of the women in their lives that they wouldn't even answer the questions. These men were completely unaware of the way they contributed to the various typecasts that confound Black women, even as they attempted to defend their race from stereotypes.

Author bell hooks would not be surprised, "No other group in America has so had their identity socialized out of existence as have Black women…when Black people are talked about the focus tends to be on Black men; and when women are talked about the focus tends to be on white women."

Very rarely are Black women celebrated for our wholeness. From our super intellectually accomplished former First Lady Michelle Obama to our super-performing athlete Serena Williams, no Black woman is spared from being cast as Sapphire, Mammy, and/or Jezebel. After leaving the White House, Michelle Obama shared a part of her experience as First Lady, "Knowing that after eight years of working really hard for this country, there are still people who won't see me for what I am because of my skin color…" she told the crowd. "Women, we endure those cuts in so many ways that we don't even know we're cut," she said, according to a report in the Denver Post. "We are living with small tiny cuts, and we are bleeding every single day. And we're still getting up."

It is no surprise that with such a diminished projection of Black women's worth, when we are violated, especially if we are poor, legal protections are slim. Legal scholar Professor Kimberle Crenshaw points out that this contributes to men who rape Black women tending to get lesser jail time than men who rape white women. "Blacks have long been portrayed as more sexual, more earthy, more gratification-oriented. These sexualized images of race intersect with norms of women's sexuality, norms that are used to distinguish good women from bad, the Madonna's from the whores."

For Black women, the colliding lanes of sexist, racist, gender-based, and classist traumatic forces reverberate at multiple levels— from the society at large to our community within to our personal family and, as the brothers on the talk show displayed, to our intimate partners. The intersectionality of these multiple oppressions adds texture and complexity to Black women's injuries. Or, in the words of sociologist and psychiatric epidemiologist Dr. Stephani Hatch, "There is something specific that being Black and woman brings to the table that you're not going to get from a Black man or a white woman."

While Black women frequently have been put in impossible situations to keep our families together and provide "good enough" parenting for our children with or without partnership, we are also persecuted for the very traits that make strong Black women successful. Indeed, escaped slave Sojourner Truth's haunting cry for respect is one that is still being echoed today.

> That man over there says that women need to be helped into carriages, and lifted over ditches, and to have the best place everywhere. Nobody ever helps me into carriages, or over mud-puddles, or gives me any best place! And ain't I a woman? Look at me! Look at my arm! I have ploughed and planted, and gathered into barns, and no man could head me! And ain't I a woman? I could work as much and eat as much as a man - when I could get it - and bear the lash as well! And ain't I a woman? I have borne thirteen children, and seen most all sold off to slavery, and when I cried out with my mother's grief, none but Jesus heard me! And ain't I a woman?

How ironic that in the American political context Black women, without recognition and resources, can always be depended upon to do the right thing to preserve democracy and freedom for all. Black women have shown this with their vote in elections in recent years. In the 2017 Alabama senate election, 65% of White women voted for the candidate with an alleged history of child sexual abuse, while 96% of African American women voted for the other candidate with no such history. And in the 2016 Presidential elections, 53% of White women voted as their 2016 presidential candidate a known misogynist with multiple allegations of sexual harassment. By comparison, 94% of Black women supported the other candidate, a woman with no such history.

Black men are also victims of gender-based oppression, but for different reasons than Black women. Whereas Black women are devalued as belonging to an overall inferior gender (female), Black men's devaluation is based upon fear of their perceived superior sexual potency, the presumption of large penis size. Black men's gender-based oppression began during the days of slavery when they were used as breeding objects to increase the pool of slaves. And post-slavery enactments such as Black codes, sharecropping, lynching, and convict leasing were used to control Black men's sexual freedom and labor because their fertility was no longer needed. The white supremacist system desired to curtail the numbers of freed Blacks, as they were perceived to be an economic hardship and no longer the driver of economic productivity.

In his book *The Tragedy of Lynching*, author Arthur Raper reported that between 1889 and 1930, 3,784 people were lynched in America, four-fifths of whom were Black. A Black man was hanged or burned approximately every four days. The most serious and common offense for lynching Black men was that they looked at white women. Lynching was justified as a means of protecting white women. Lynching, and the need to protect white women from Black male's bodies in public water spaces and preserve their fragile femininity, is the central theme of Richard Wright's essay "Big Boy Leaves Home" in his 1938 collection *Uncle Tom's Children*. Black women, some of whom were pregnant, were also lynched, though at a lesser rate than Black men. They were oftentimes lynched as being accomplices to men.

In her treatise on melanin confrontation *The Cress Theory of Color Confrontation and Racism*, renowned African American Psychiatrist Dr. Frances Cress Welsing put forth an argument to explain why this fear of the Black man was so pervasive that it led to the high lynching ratios. She argued that biology played a large role in stoking that fear. According to Dr. Cress Welsing, the traits of Blacks and other people of color are dominant to recessive white genetic traits. As a result, Black men carry a weapon (Freudian symbolism of the penis as a gun) to destroy white genetic expression and the purity of the white race, which makes them the most threatening race and gender by far to white people. Dr. Cress Welsing points out that Black women always have Black children, even if fathered by white men. Black men however, when they father children with white women, will father Black children. Black men therefore became weapons that could destroy the white race.

One might argue that the current over-policing and incarceration of Black men is a modern day form of lynching, together with state-sponsored killing of unarmed Black men. If Black men are locked away or dead, they cannot melanize the white race. And of course, in many of these instances past and current, whites are not held accountable and Blacks are blamed for making whites have to kill them.

Black male sexuality has always been a source of implicit angst in the psyche of white supremacists. Dr. Arnold James, psychologist and expert in Black male psychology, stated:

> Facetiously, I wonder what whites say at the white convention to young white girls to make then so scared of Black men. What is the message being given that becomes part of the cultural message that Black men should be feared? Remember, during slavery the "big penis" as much as it was feared, had a lot of capital worth–it could make babies to add to the labor pool, so it had value even though it was feared as a more potent sexual object for white women.

Another form of subjugation and destruction of the Black body dates all the way back to slavery times: the horrific use of male and female bodies for medical experimentation and/or coercive punishment and reproductive control. Between 1845 and 1849, Dr. Marion Sims—referred to by some as the father of obstetrics gynecology—experimented on Black women slaves to find a surgical cure for vesicovaginal fistulas. These women were operated upon without consent and without anesthesia. In the 1990s, judges gave women convicted of child abuse or those who used drugs during their pregnancy a "choice" of prison or Norplant, a provider dependent, five-year-long-acting, progesterone-based contraceptive.

Several legislatures soon thereafter tried to introduce legislation that demanded low-income women of color who received government financial assistance either use Norplant or lose their benefits. Others proposed giving financial incentives to women who 'chose' Norplant. Currently and continuing the long history of eugenics, Long Acting Reversible Contraceptives (LARC)—IUDs or Implants—and Depo-Provera injections are being disproportionately targeted at young Black women. These women are usually poorly consented and given limited information and access to women-controlled contraceptive methods. This prescription continues despite accumulating evidence that shows impairment in immune system functioning and increased risk of HIV infection in progestin-dominant drugs, as laid out in a recent paper by Erica Gollub and Zena Stein. Similar scientific transgressions have been launched against Black men. Most infamously, the Tuskegee study "Tuskegee Study of Untreated Syphilis in the Negro male," conducted jointly by the US Public Health Service and Tuskegee Institute, is a historic national disgrace that lasted from 1932–1972. In this 40-year unethical medical atrocity, 400 Black men with syphilis were fooled into thinking that they were being treated. The researchers abused these Black men to facilitate their goal of studying the natural history and progression of the disease. Even after a cure (penicillin) was found, the researchers refused to break the research protocol and treat them.

Regardless of the callous admonitions that we are "pulling the race card again," there continues to be many current day versions of some of the well-documented historical incidents of social and structural racism leveled against Black society. In light of our own desire to move past pain and not dwell on adversity, it can be extremely difficult—without seeming to lean on the easy crutch of the "race card"—to explain the pressure and struggle we endure daily. It is invisible and hard to name at times, too blatant to be true at others. Healing the Black mind and body requires continuous interrogation and working through the evidence of how structural systems of race and gender-based oppression and violence have scarred us.

Chapter 6

Injurious Community Experience

African culture has always been rooted in communal collaboration, a norm that persists in its offspring throughout the diaspora around the world. Neal Lester, a humanities professor at Arizona State University who specializes in African-American literary studies, says of the well-worn saying it takes a village to raise a child, "The essence of the proverb speaks to a certain worldview that challenges Western individualism." No matter its overuse, this proverb highlights how the tearing apart and bulldozing of African American communities wounds the will and soul of a people who historically have prospered in communal environments.

As was noted by the Scottish Development Center for Mental Health, "How society works at every level influences the way people feel about themselves. And how people feel influences how well society functions." Indeed, Black ancestral culture is rooted in collectivity, and white supremacy's systems of denigration and subjugation have been and are injurious not only to individual Black bodies, but also to the structures in the collective spaces where we are born, live, work, play, and worship. It has severely limited the structures' capacity to serve as protective factors for our communities. Historic injustices, plus current day socio-economic inequities and disparities, have relegated many of us to environments with poor housing, education, nutrition, and air quality; little access to outdoor recreation and healthcare; and limited economic opportunities.

In 2007, in the aftermath of Hurricane Katrina, I served as expert psychiatric witness in the case of Andrew v HUD. In the midst of the severe housing crisis post-Katrina, New Orleans public housing had been bulldozed and destroyed. Numerous poor, mostly female-headed, African American households lost their homes. In many studies of post-disaster mental health, loss of housing has been shown to be one of the key factors associated with the development of PTSD. Not surprisingly, a longitudinal study led by public health expert Christina Paxson of 532 low-income mothers from New Orleans pre- and post-Katrina found that home damage was an especially important predictor of chronic post-traumatic stress syndrome.

In my preparation for the case, I interviewed six of the plaintiffs, four of whom were living in trailers in New Orleans and two of whom had relocated to Houston. All six were suffering from PTSD, directly attributable to the deliberate destruction of public housing and the loss of their homes. They were keenly aware that no one in decision-making roles had their best interest at heart nor cared about the plaintiffs' physical and mental wellbeing. When the case was eventually thrown out unheard on a technicality, it added more salt to their wounds and confirmed everything they believed about the system.

What happened in New Orleans post-Katrina is not an isolated experience. It is part of a long history of Black communities being dismantled. Institutional racism not only destroys the vulnerable aspects of our culture, it has wreaked havoc and physical destruction on place-based Black neighborhoods and decimated many flourishing communities. Greenwood community in Northern Tulsa brings such a recollection. In 1921 a white woman reported that a black man sexually assaulted her, and up to 300 African Americans lost their lives when the town was looted and burned to the ground. At the time, Greenwood was the wealthiest Black community in America and was affectionately known as "Black Wall Street." And Rosewood, a thriving Black community in Florida, was burned down in 1923 after a white woman, once again, said that a Black man had attacked her.

Isabel Wilkerson, in her Pulitzer prize-winning novel *The Warmth of Other Suns*, painfully depicts a bold narrative of the Great Migration—that of Black immigration from the South. This is a heart-breaking tale of Black people in the early 1900s that were forced to escape the brutality of the South and search for freedom elsewhere in their own land. This is exasperatingly similar to the journey almost a century later of displaced Black people in New Orleans seeking refuge after Hurricane Katrina. In both instances, Black people were treated and perceived as other, refugees, and not welcome in their homeland. Remedies and recourse that should have been available to and provided for New Orleans after the natural disaster were dismal and fell way short of just and humane. No concern was shown on the governmental level about the price that the migration and ultimate loss of community would cost their overall wellbeing.

And yet even more current, the narrative is once again being played on repeat in Puerto Rico after Hurricane Maria hit on Sept 20, 2017, devastating most of the island's infrastructure. Puerto Ricans, Americans by birth, a significant number of whom are mixtures of brown and Black people, do not seem to have been deemed worthy of an equitable recovery. They have not received the amount of governmental resources and sympathy as occurred in Texas and

Florida post Hurricanes Harvey and Irma respectively. Close to 50% of the island remained without power months after the hurricane. Threats to end FEMA support were frequent for a variety of services the island still needed to survive, and Puerto Rico's stalled and painful recovery has fallen onto the back pages of media reports.

What is the long-term effect of this type of PTSD when it goes untreated? Traumatized individuals operate from fear rather than hope; feel fragmented and dissociated rather than whole; feel numb rather than alive; feel paranoid rather than safe. The popular saying, "untreated trauma leads to drama" is true for individuals as well as communities. One forced migration, one evacuation, one repatriation, builds upon the other. The capacity of communities and the people who inhabit them to be efficacious and resilient becomes diminished by persistent racial traumas, unfairness, and inequity. As was noted by the Prevention Institute in Oakland, California, chronic trauma and adversity destroy communities in their totality—the built environment, the socio-cultural environment (social networks, trust, social norms, capacity for advocacy), and the economic environment.

Living in environmental conditions reflective of chronic adversity (poverty, racism) is akin to living in a perpetual cauldron of toxic stress. When extenuating acute shocks occur, the trauma is only compounded. Katrina is one such example of an acute stressor that exacerbated the chronic adversities and toxic stress that previously existed. The current Black experience in many other oppressed communities—African American, brown, or sexual/gender non-conforming/non-normative—is a "Katrina" happening over and over again, but bearing a different name. Each of these community's strength and health becomes further and further depressed and diluted with each implosion.

Razing our communities has not always required the existence of the urgency of a criminal complaint or a natural disaster as a catalyst. Their destruction has also been meticulously planned and executed by those in power. Social psychiatrist and scholar Dr. Mindy Fullilove describes how under the guise of "slum clearance" in the 1950s, many urban landscapes were deliberately demolished to make way for highways. In a double twist of insult to injury, the highways were needed to provide access to the white suburbs because whites had fled there (i.e. white flight) to avoid integration. This practice rooted itself into the urban planning ethos, resulting in "forced serial displacement," which she describes as "the repetitive, coercive upheaval of groups." Fullilove and fellow psychiatrist Rodrick Wallace theorize that such displacement "sets up a dynamic process that includes an increase in interpersonal and structural violence, an inability to react in a timely fashion to patterns of threat and opportunity, and a cycle of fragmentation as a result of the first two."

Fullilove and Wallace point out that segregation, redlining, urban renewal, planned shrinkage/catastrophic disinvestment, deindustrialization, mass criminalization, gentrification, HOPE VI revitalization of dilapidated public housing into mixed income housing, and the foreclosure crisis are the mechanisms by which African Americans are continuously, institutionally displaced. Fullilove argues that neighborhood rupturing not only physically uproots people, it leaves the affected groups disoriented, nostalgic, and alienated by creating "root shock"—a traumatic stress reaction related to the destruction of one's emotional ecosystem. She states, however, that the Black community does not fully grasp that serial forced displacement is what has happened to us:

Losing our neighborhoods, and not just once but also

many times, has undermined the civil rights victories that we won. It doesn't matter what life stage you are—you need that stable, loving environment to help you do the task of that stage and move on to the next stage. Girls, boys…no one can have a healthy life without stability. According to the Ericksonian model of continuous development throughout the life cycle, we move into old age and into the position of being elders in the community. But who's going to teach us how to do that if the community is torn apart and we have all this terrible excess mortality and elders die before they can teach us how to be elders.

Place matters—where one lives matters; zip codes matter.

In the book, *American Apartheid*, Douglas S. Massey and Nancy A. Denton describe how deep and persistent segregation and separation, or hyper-segregation, remain a fact of American life and lead to a host of social ills and health concerns. It correlates to why Black Americans die at higher rates than whites from most causes– AIDS, cardiovascular diseases (diabetes, hypertension), homicide, and perinatal disorders.

Socially, the loss of collectivity and neighborliness in economically depressed areas often lead to them being abandoned by the Black middle class. These "inner-city" neighborhoods are bereft of those with the advocacy tools and resources to demand equity, so they struggle on the margins with extremes of poverty and violence. What remains after "Black flight" is a more intense concentration of the negative aspects of these neighborhoods: survival-based "hood culture and logic."

Dr. Mindy Fullilove warns:

One of the great myths in America is that everybody is middle class. Whatever that means—it means nothing. Which basically, in the Black community, means, you're a white collar worker as opposed to working in a factory, which probably means you have some nasty government job. Or, in these more recent times, you've become a lawyer or a doctor, so that's really high status. It doesn't mean that you have any wealth or any money. Because, we don't have any wealth nor do we have a lot of money. And it doesn't mean you're separated from the poor. The thing is that everybody has someone in their family somebody who's in prison, somebody who's crazy, somebody who's addicted, somebody who's been brutally harmed…so the tensions of all this tearing at the world are not far from the circle of middle class. So really the distance between the richest Black people and the poorest Black people is much smaller than the distance between the richest white people and the poorest…and most Black people are pretty close in income. So if somebody goes to prison, it ripples through the world of the middle class person so I think there's a kind of desperation.

When the mark of success in the community is that the brightest, smartest, most capable have left—escaped really—there is no powerful internal savior left to lead the rebuilding of the community and to nurture the reversal of years of mental disease from the inside out. Its damaged state then becomes prevalently seen, stereotyped, and projected by the media as the totality of Black culture. All the while, the positive aspects of those economically marginalized who find creative ways to exist, survive, and find joy are cast as aberrations to the rule, with the exception of those aspects that can be exploited for mass consumption—fashion, music, athleticism.

Some Black scholars who grew up in segregated America, like

my late husband Dr. Walter Shervington, have argued that Black culture lost the collectivity and purpose that existed during segregation—that which had rendered strong resistance and built resilience in the face of oppression. The socio-cultural fallout of the end of segregation was that we could and would finally "move on up to the East side." But even if the Black middle to upper classes have bought into the delusion that wealth and class were protective factors against racism—the delusion of integration—white America has shown them otherwise. Take, for example, the racist vandalism of basketball star LeBron James' mansion in Los Angeles. Or, the incident in which esteemed Harvard Professor Henry Louis "Skip" Gates was arrested under suspicion of breaking into his own home in Cambridge.

As upwardly mobile Blacks began to gain more access to previously off-limits systems such as education, economics, and housing, for the most part they have not turned that benefit back into the community. Dr. Walter Shervington used to reminisce nostalgically about how the Black community in Baltimore, so proud of him for being the first from their community to attend an Ivy League university, would fundraise every year to send him back to school with pocket money. Or how his father got his loan to a start his private practice from the head numbers-runner that lived in their segregated apartment building. But many who received these early community-helping hands have distanced themselves from the macro level collective Black identity that was a unifier during segregation and have kept clear of, rather than challenging, the dominant negative stereotypes coming out of the vacuum of the disrupted communities. In the long run, this has left the most vulnerable and less-mobile Black people to fend for themselves.

Ultimately, the power, passion, and most importantly, empathy and understanding, are taken to other areas, usually white, where the successful can continue to grow. But within these new communities, I have treated many who struggle with the feelings of being outsiders looking in. They live with subtle or vocal castigations of being either "oreos" or not Black enough socially, and battle the need to work harder, longer, and better to keep their economic place secure. The ties that kept them stable become frayed—back in our "inner city" communities, they who have left are callously dismissed as sellouts by the weakest of the weak, as the name callers in turn slip further and further down the ladder of self-healing possibility. There is no need to condemn those who have left. Their survival sometimes depends upon it. However, the vacuum their presence leaves is damage that cannot be ignored. And their feelings of alienation in their new communities create yet other issues.

I have observed how some middle class Black youth, unaware of the complexity and rich texture of Black culture, have adopted the negative stereotypes of Blackness as their identity. Earlier in the Introduction I mentioned MM, the young man I worked with while he was in juvenile detention. He is an example of the flip side of the destroyed community. MM was the son of a very wealthy Black California family. His early education was in private white schools, as a result of which he socialized only with white children. As he entered adolescence—the period when we all start to question who we are—the façade of being a part of a community fell away. His white friends and their families began to shun him, and he no longer felt accepted in their circles, especially around their daughters.

In his attempt to begin to formulate a Black identity, he turned to the young people who lived down the hill and literally across the tracks. The negative, survival-based aspects of "hood" life had been fed to him by the media as authentic Black masculinity. When his "new Black friends" from across the tracks decided to rob a store, he was all in. His decision was not based on economic need like the others, but on his emotional need to have community, to belong. It turned violent as he waited in what was to be the getaway car, his parents' Rolls Royce, no less. MM, with all his economic advantages and despite his parent's "escape" from the hood, was charged with being an accomplice to robbery and attempted murder.

The few places where African Americans have carved out healthy communities where they can find the comfort of being amongst their own are, at times, marginalized or invaded by whites with no deference to the need for this type of environment. A poignant example was two young white women walking into a café on Howard University's campus, a historically Black university founded in 1867 and a long-standing African American community. The women wore hats touting the Donald Trump campaign slogan, "Make America Great Again." It did not go well. The welcome that has been extended to the many non-minorities who access the campus for various reasons was immediately retracted because of the controversial message on the baseball hats—for very obvious reasons to everyone but the teenage women and many like them in social media who have the luxury of ignorance.

Whatever our reaction to this kind of button-pushing incident or the more blatant show of Neo-Nazi White Klan Supremacy "making America great (white) again" and "Unite the Right" rally recently in Charlottesville, what hasn't changed is white people feeling they belong and can do anything anywhere and everywhere, while Black people have to explain the necessity for the few areas of community comfort we have. That notion perpetuates whether as vocal as it roared in the trans-Atlantic slave trade or as subtle as the pinprick needling that would influence two young women to feel they have the right to flaunt a controversial political inclination in the sanctity of a historically Black university campus. It is such a privilege to be able to walk the streets of this country and assume you belong anywhere you are. Sensitivity to the fact that this privilege belongs only to white people, regardless of the socio-economic standing of their community, is lost on many and denied by others.

Experiencing that lack of sensitivity is daily life for Blacks today. In Black Rage, Cobbs and Grier described cultural depression as "sadness and intimacy with misery." It speaks to the wound open in not only Black individuals, but in Black communities everywhere. Black culture, that emanating from the Black collective survival arsenal, is constantly pushed beyond the "stress yield point." These injuries manifest in Black people's relationships with Self and with each other and create suffering that ripples through our homes, our families, and our communities. They manifest in new cultural norms that develop in our ravaged communities, such as our young people thinking it's okay to resolve interpersonal conflict and feelings of being disrespected with a bullet. These new norms reflect cultural grief, hopelessness, despair, and depression. They are not Black genetic traits.

Just like economic flight and social mobility take our gifted and successful, the effects of learned reliance on violence are multitude on the community. The "mean streets," the "concrete jungle" to which many of our children have been relegated, has left some hardened and soulless. There are no elders or neighbors to love, direct, and correct them as they try to navigate the traumas and toxic stress that come with the harsh realities of current day poverty. As one such young man told me, "If only I had people to talk to me and help me; those kids doing wrong, they were more than happy to lead me astray like them." With no village to raise them, and especially so in the absence of good enough parenting, some of our youth deal with conflict and disappointment through the lens of the stereotypic illusions of manhood, pride, and respectability. This not only decimates our ranks of young people—who should grow up to continue and carry the community—but also destroys those left behind to pick up the pieces.

It is always said, "a parent shouldn't have to bury their child." But so many of our parents are burying their children. Here are the words of one such parent left with a permanent hole in his heart, inflicted upon him and his family by one of our lost sons, one who perhaps was never raised to feel that his life, ergo no other life, truly mattered:

> I've been thinking, "who are the other hundreds of parents who lost their sons to violence?" And, I've been wondering, "what does it mean to revisit the experience of loss with others?" Recently I met a mother who also lost her son—we hugged, and I melted into her; I could not let go.

> I've been reading a lot of James Baldwin recently–It feels like "proofing through the fire," wherein difficult experiences create a deeper purpose. That's what my journey has been. Not a day passes by when I don't think of him. Sometimes I wonder if I should move to Fiji. But soon, all those brown boys would remind me of him. I constantly think about how to honor his loss and have it inform what needs to be done.

> I realize that I have to get honest about the permanency of the change. I wonder, why did he not listen to me. There is a bitterness connected to the unauthorized loss in my life. I wonder, what went wrong in the life of the person who ended my son's life. For seriously, how do you kill your

peer. And it makes me think of safety. But, as long as we have been in this country, Black people have not been safe. The question that keeps coming up is how to protect your young Black son? What does it mean to be safe as a Black boy or man? How do we make safety? We are in a public health crisis—if this were a virus killing us, would more actions been taken by now?

I have been talking with his friends. I ask them, what should we do? What should they do? They say they don't know—so, they just go on living as if things are normal. We are in the middle of it and we never have these conversations. We need to be talking about how to change this culture of violence—it is so endemic, the language with which young people communicate endearment is violent at times—slapping, hitting each other as a sign of love. We have cultivated spaces that are anti-healing, not loving, and not conducive to healthy youth development. We therefore need to cultivate safe environments.

Daily I think about how to find intentional joy—how to build it in. From sitting at home eating popcorn and watching movies, taking a hot bath or being with friends. I am discovering that my deeper purpose is joy and authentic justice. For me, authentic justice is an extension of my desire to allow people to flower. I want to remove the barriers and instead replace them with investments in positive development. That's what my community did for me when I was growing up. So even though there was domestic violence in my home, the community made sure there were positive supports for me to navigate the pain.

I want to create spaces where our children can be "loved up" and not penalized when they screw up, all the while holding them accountable. I want responsible citizens to reimagine and recreate a vision of a better society. That is what my criminal reform work is about. Rather than extend the punitive jail spaces, can we instead build a garden. We do know that punishment alone is not therapeutic. When these folks get out, nothing has changed in them, and they go back to the old hurt behaviors. We are in the fight for our lives—it's not just about these monuments of the confederate generals. The biggest monument to the confederacy is the jail.

The one-year anniversary of his death is coming soon. I have blocked off that date and a few others from my schedule. I told my staff to act as if I were out of the country. I want to say yes to caring for myself and not always being available to others.

Dr. Arnold James shared the following perspective as he and I attempted to more deeply interrogate the root cause of the current crisis of Black male aggression towards each other:

For the most part, Black men have not been taught the psychological/emotional language to identify emotions and employ effective problem solving behaviors to discharge their uncomfortable feelings and make sense of painful experiences. Being vulnerable means being able to identify pain, accept the pain and believe that you can tolerate it. The message we give to young boys is, "you are not supposed to cry; if you do, you will be labeled a punk, sissy, or some disparaging term to question maleness." This leads to disruption of emotional development. This disruption disallows the natural tendency to feel and produces emotional trauma. And eventually such trauma when imprinted on the brain can lead to aggressive fantasies that are acted out in violence.

What are the foundational experiences for Black boys so that they can develop a healthy masculinity? How do we address arrested emotional development? This is not just about modeling testosterone; it should be about re-parenting and recalibration of the young men's empathic failures. By empathic failure I mean the inability to meet an important emotional need at critical times in a person's development. All people need to be loved and attended to, to feel they matter, to feel safe, to be allowed to be intellectually curious, in consistent, cohesive, and predictable environment—too much chaos and unpredictable movement causes trauma. These failures occur when caretakers are not able to communicate to their child that they empathize with the disillusionment they feel when they have to gradually let go of their infantile narcissism and omnipotence in order to develop and take their place in the social order. When empathic failures occur, children have difficulty developing healthy self-esteem, self-soothing, tolerating tension, and being emphatic with others. Very importantly, Black boys need to feel they matter.

People that look just like us die and there are no consequences. If I have a need to matter and manage my pain without any direction or modeling of pro-social behaviors, I might draw attention to myself to not make me feel like a little man who does not matter, so I come with hyperactivity, or I make a baby, or make trouble. When you are not made aware of your worth, when no one asks you what you want to be when you grow up, when no one asked you that question when you were ages three or four years, "what's your ambition?" then you do not know it's important. If you are hearing it for the first time in high school, it's too late. Another source of empathic failures for Black boys is being made to feel shame and have reduced value of their Black skin—almost as if we cannot love them unconditionally because of their Black skin.

We need to instill hope—it's going to be okay. We need to allow for mourning, the time needed to say goodbye to infantile needs. We need transitional objects to give us continuity, versus abrupt stops and starts. We need to be able to internalize a moral code of how to be. We need to feel connected. Intergenerational poverty leads to trauma in little boys, for it sometimes creates a limited view of Self and possibilities. It is not easy to motivate your offspring when you are struggling every day to survive. I have noticed how in the South Black boys have to grow up faster than those I have seen in the Northeast, especially those who grew up in the suburbs. It is very different if you grew up able to ride your bicycle and have your parents drive you to activities, versus having to take the bus and struggle to get everywhere. Also, what does your village reflect? What do you learn to value?

Emboldened reconstructive policies and actions are needed if we are to turn the tide on community trauma. The work has begun, and it is upon each of us to do our individual work as well as to support organizations such as The Prevention Institute, which provides us with a blueprint to:

- Reclaim public space that is appealing to residents and reflective of their culture; this suggests that we remove problematic monuments that were erected to celebrate white supremacy

- Rebuild and maintain public spaces that encourage positive social interactions and relationships, as well as healthy behaviors and activities
- Improve economic opportunities for youth and adults by improving education so that college enrollment can increase, and provide job training and placement for non-college bound youth
- Provide job training and job readiness for formerly incarcerated members of the community
- And, very importantly, resist the rising pressures of gentrification

Chapter 7
Self-Love

> Self-care and truly loving myself has allowed me to clear my mind to make better decisions in my life.
> ~ Self-care group participant

As a people we have depended on our ability to survive. As such the value in our being durable in spirit is not in question. We are here despite all that we have met with decade after decade! But the true challenge is for us to move beyond surviving and into thriving, both as individuals and as a community. And only with deliberate, strategic actions and intentions to facilitate healing can we move our existence into its truer potential for vibrancy. Healing begins with the recognition that we are damaged, that we are wounded. No matter how counterintuitive it feels, healing begins to happen when we give room to grief, sadness, disappointment, fear, and anger.

Healing is the process of optimizing the repair of one's state of wholeness after an injury. It is the caring process of bringing the body back into a state of recovery, relaxation, and joy. No prescription for health can be written before what ails us is identified, and identified in all areas of our being. Because in order to repair and heal the whole Self, there has to be integration of body, mind, and spirit essence. The wounds and burdens that we have borne have left scars around these three areas that comprise our total existence. We have to reach back into the pain and be intentional in using our memory as a weapon against the conflicted unconscious, both individual and collective, that directs our current Self.

For six months I convened a working group of over fifty community members to explore the barriers to the growth and wellbeing of Black people. We utilized the Social Ecological Model theory as the basis of analysis, which considers the complex interplay between individual, interpersonal, community, and societal factors and recognizes that individual behavior is shaped by and shapes the context in which people live. The following are the issues we gained consensus on:

- At the societal level—interpersonal and institutional racism; the prison industrial complex (racial profiling; over-policing; mass incarceration); poverty and lack of economic and educational opportunities; and negative racial stereotyping
- At the community/neighborhood level–lack of positive Black male role models; drug infestation and low prosocial norms about drug use; violence; failing schools; minimal recreational outlets; cultural stigma regarding mental health services; inadequate access to health services and resultant health disparities; loss of group collectivity and resilience; substandard and inadequate housing; and poverty
- At the interpersonal level—empathic failures of parental figures who are unable to meet their child's basic need to attach, feel loved, nurtured, and protected; traumatic experiences due to sexual, physical and sexual abuse, neglect, and parental loss
- At the individual level—difficulty mentalizing a positive "self-concept," especially for males; low self-esteem and self-regard; identity confusion; lack of sufficient emotional intelligence to resolve feelings of sadness, hurt,

anger, fear; maladaptive behaviors—violence, substance
abuse; low capacity for intimacy, vulnerability, and love;
and, diminished capacity to embrace leadership

Engaging in this deeper understanding of why and how our
mental and physical bodies are battered and wrecked makes it easier
to explore and discover what we can do to heal our clipped wings
and broken spirit. Such is the African principle of Sankofa—we
cannot move forward into the future without knowing our past.
Otherwise, we are bound not only to repeat the dysfunction, but also
to pass it on via individual attachments, in our social networks, and
through socio-cultural norms and beliefs to future generations.

We begin to find our personal reparations by committing
ourselves to the time it will take, the space we must give ourselves,
and the means we need to embark on a journey to the true nature of
our total being. Derek Walcott, the late great St. Lucian author,
captures the journey back to Self in his poem:

Love After Love

The time will come
when, with elation
you will greet yourself arriving
at your own door, in your own mirror
and each will smile at the other's welcome,

and say, sit here. Eat.
You will love again the stranger who was your self.
Give wine. Give bread. Give back your heart
to itself, to the stranger who has loved you

all your life, whom you ignored
for another, who knows you by heart.

Take down the love letters from the bookshelf,

the photographs, the desperate notes,
peel your own image from the mirror.
Sit. Feast on your life.

The process can simply begin with a deep inhale—deep enough to create stillness; still enough to begin to name your pain and conjure up the courage to tolerate whatever vulnerability might arise. A good jumping off point is the very simple self-interrogation, "Where is the pain lodged in my psyche? How have I been holding on to it in my body? How has my spirit been broken?"

Unfortunately, as we bump up against our inner conflicts, we oftentimes create resistance and defenses to protect ourselves against the anxiety of knowing. This is when many adopt the mantra "keep it moving" in order to avoid the discomfort that comes with accepting the reality that brought on our pain. We fear lessening our inner noise and sitting still. This arises out of intense apprehension that memories of past hurt will be intolerable. But it won't—it works as a crucial phase to move through and not an endpoint. Naming, reflecting, feeling, and uncovering shines the light on our dark spaces and helps us to release that which haunts us, similar to when a physical abscess is lanced and the pus drains out

And if we don't do the work and begin the naming and feeling, we risk continuing to infect our entire system if/when the abscess spontaneously bursts, which is bound to happen if we allow the pus to build up. Langston Hughes used this dramatic metaphor in his bold and eloquent 1951 poem, "A Dream Deferred," to draw attention to the rawness and consequences of our unhealed lives. Half a century later, the risk of infection has not significantly lessened and should not be ignored.

A Dream Deferred

What happens to a dream deferred?

> Does it dry up
> like a raisin in the sun?
> Or fester like a sore—
> And then run?
> Does it stink like rotten meat?
> Or crust and sugar over—
> like a syrupy sweet?
>
> Maybe it just sags
> like a heavy load.
>
> *Or does it explode?*

Lancing the abscesses in us is the dynamic process of recovering our sacredness. It requires releasing the woundedness, all that which would otherwise stagnate our growth. All in all, the healing journey requires us to be vulnerable in the face of our pain and our joy, and ultimately in the face of our unavoidable death. Healing the Black mind and body requires that we slow down, stop, look, listen, and trust that we will be able to act from a place of deep knowing. Healing requires us to live from the space of "as is" and dealing with our reality, not "as if," when things are not as they are but how we want them to be.

Diving in and understanding how we were derailed from our dreams and ambitions allows us to get distance from the pain and eventually find freedom. Being vulnerable, softening, and opening our hearts is the portal to what is so eloquently and succinctly stated by Kahlil Gibran, "Your joy is the breaking of the shell that encloses your pain." Understanding the interplay between our feelings, thoughts, and physical sensations teaches us how to better regulate our lives. Our feelings, especially when they have a charge on them, negative or positive, are what underpin the extent to which we hold on to our thoughts.

Buddhist scholar Robert Wright argues that our feelings are what "glue" our thoughts to our consciousness. Understanding and releasing old hurts, frustrations, and disappointments teaches us important life lessons and helps unchain us from our past. We do not have to become prisoners or victims, or worse, perpetrators. We do not have to suffer. In order to get there, however, we have to allow our heart to be broken, so that it can open—journey through the darkness and open up to all the potential that is beyond pain. Indeed, tasting but not lingering in the dark side of life helps us to move into the light. This means we become aware of the masks that we wear and gradually take them off, practicing self-care along the way.

As we acknowledge the parts of our life that are filled with pain and suffering, we maintain the healing journey with this continued commitment to our self-care. Self-care is the ongoing journey of deepening our self-discovery and nurturing the true core of our total being, caring for each of the three parts discussed earlier—physical, mental, and essence (spirit, soul). On the physical level, self-care demands that we optimize the operating efficiency of the physical body through healthy nutrition, aerobic fitness, and relaxation. Mentally, we must increase our self-awareness through uncovering and witnessing the machinations of our mind. And in caring for our essence (spirit, soul), we must penetrate and connect to the deep mystery of life: "Who and what am I?"

Self-care builds our personal resilience, our ability to resist, absorb, accommodate to, transform, and/or recover when facing life's challenges. In other words, the ability to bounce back, build one's Self back better, and spring forward into new opportunities. Overall self-care requires us to: set priorities and realistic goals; acknowledge ambivalence and contradictions; and find balance between work, pleasure, retreat, and communion. Healing starts from the outside in, from now to the beginning and back again to now, and to a hopeful future to come.

Self-care and self-healing will allow us to travel into the interior of our being and come to know our truer Self, the one we have always desired to become. And when we do, just maybe we will discover that this is where the life force resides in us, which will restore our confidence in what we know to be our truth as Black people. Healing mind, body, and spirit is a love journey back to the Self, a dance within the beauty and awe of the universe. The healing journey helps us discover our oneness with the divine and our connection to all beings. Healing and self-care behoove us to move beyond our superficial boundaries and connect with all that the universe has surrounded us with: her plants, her animals, her oceans, her earth, and her sky. We are not alone on this journey. It is a lesson in learning how dependent we are on each other.

After working on a self-care initiative with a group of social justice leaders in New Orleans for the past two years, one of the most powerful lessons I have learned is that self-care becomes more achievable when we are in communities that give us a safe space of refuge from anti-blackness, where together we can affirm: "I matter, We matter." These are places and spaces wherein we gather, listen to each other, re-envision, imagine, and dream up our liberation. bell hooks referred to this as "homeplace," a place to decolonize our minds and perceive our full humanity and our wholeness. A true "homeplace" rejects and repairs what Black-on-Black violence signifies—the projection onto each other of the loss of the sacredness of our being. Healing our wounded spirit by recognizing our own and each other's sanctity in the here and now is the true and radical revolution and journey back to Self and each other!

Chapter 8

Mental Self-Care

How do we reclaim the power, sacredness and worth of our colored selves?

How do we stand tall in the crooked room?

How do we reconcile beauty and divinity within our Self?

How do we overcome the many years of intergenerational transmission of trauma that have negatively impacted our present sense of Self?

How do we not live the pain of our forbearers?

How do we heal the damage?

How do we finally reclaim pride in our negritude?

As I've shared, the beginning of the journey toward wellbeing starts with recognizing that our mind, body and/or spirit are broken and hurting. Such recognition comes with quieting our minds sufficiently so that we can begin the process of introspection, of going in and searching inwards. By going inwards, we increase our conscious awareness of how our feelings, especially the negative ones—sadness, fear, shame, disgust, anger—influence our thoughts and behaviors and manifest as dysfunctional patterns, which results in impacting how we turn up for life and perceive our Self and our identity. And, of course, how we relate to others.

In order to go inwards, however, we have to become more aware of how we distract our Self from our Self and live our life on the surface, away from who we truly are. Some of these distractions come in the form of media, celebrity worship, overwork, and minding others' business rather than our own. Another way in which we distract ourselves from the reality of life as it unfolds is through psychological defense mechanisms. These are some of the common defenses that our ego uses to minimize our anxieties:

- **Denial**. Refusal to deal with and accept reality and/or facts
- **Projection**. Attributing unacceptable feelings or thoughts to another
- **Reaction formation**. Converting undesirable thoughts or impulses into their opposite
- **Regression**. Shifting one's pattern of behaviors to an earlier stage of psychological development, e.g. an adolescent reverting to infantile behaviors
- **Repression**. Burying unacceptable thoughts into the unconscious
- **Acting out**. Using behaviors to express one's feelings
- **Dissociation**. Splitting off and detaching one's emotional experiences from one's identity

Some of the healthier, mature defenses are:

- **Suppression**. A conscious decision to delay dealing with difficult situation in order to cope with current reality
- **Anticipation**. Planning ahead
- **Altruism**. Satisfying needs through helping others
- **Humor**. Finding joy in laughter
- **Sublimation**. Acting out unacceptable impulses by converting them to more acceptable ones

Do you recognize any of these processes in you? How have these defenses contributed to how you compile your present life?

In order to find out, it's necessary to engage in some form of ongoing introspection and self-questioning. Be aware, however, that if you find yourself blocking the process of deepening your self-awareness, unacknowledged and/or unhealed trauma could be the reason why. And, although the concept of trauma as a source of mental distress has now become popularized and over-referenced like other psychological constructs such as bullying, triggers, and resilience, as Black people, we are at heightened for risk developing traumatic stress disorders. This is because, in addition to the traumatic encounters that can normally result from simply being alive, we also experience trauma from living in a society that devalues our existence.

Trauma results from having an encounter that leaves an individual feeling overwhelmed and unable to cope. Unaddressed trauma can negatively impact mental and physical health. Before the age of 18 years, chronic and compounding childhood maltreatment, which Bessel van der Kolk and colleagues have labeled as developmental trauma, occurs within the context of disrupted or impaired attachment with primary caretakers. This results in a complex picture of dysregulation of emotions, cognitions, relatedness to Self and others, and identity disturbances in children. Once again, examples of such adverse childhood experiences (ACE) as discussed in chapter four are: physical, sexual or emotional abuse or neglect, and/or living in a household where there was dysfunction due to parental substance abuse, mental illness, divorce, incarceration, or death. Other sources of developmental trauma are war and community trauma.

The following conventional Adverse Childhood Experiences

questionnaire can help you assess your status. Please note, however, that The Philadelphia version of the ACE survey, developed initially by the Institute for Safe Families and later by the Health Federation, expanded this conventional ACE questionnaire to include questions on: witnessing violence, living in unsafe neighborhoods, experiencing racism, living in foster care, and experiencing bullying.

ACE Score Sheet

Prior to your 18th birthday:

1. Did a parent or other adult in the household often or very often swear at you, insult you, put you down, or humiliate you? or Act in a way that made you afraid that you might be physically hurt?

   No ___ If Yes, enter 1 ___

2. Did a parent or other adult in the household often or very often push, grab, slap, or throw something at you? or Ever hit you so hard that you had marks or were injured?

   No ___ If Yes, enter 1 ___

3. Did an adult or person at least 5 years older than you ever touch or fondle you or have you touch their body in a sexual way? or Attempt or actually have oral, anal, or vaginal intercourse with you?

   No ___ If Yes, enter 1 ___

4. Did you often or very often feel that no one in your family loved you or thought you were important or

special? or Your family didn't look out for each other, feel close to each other, or support each other?

No ____ If Yes, enter 1 ____

5. Did you often or very often feel that you didn't have enough to eat, had to wear dirty clothes, and had no one to protect you? or Your parents were too drunk or high to take care of you or take you to the doctor if you needed it?

No ____ If Yes, enter 1 ____

6. Were your parents ever separated or divorced?

No ____ If Yes, enter 1 ____

7. Was either your mother or your stepmother often or very often pushed, grabbed, slapped, or had something thrown at her? or Sometimes, often, or very often kicked, bitten, hit with a fist, or hit with something hard? or Ever repeatedly hit over at least a few minutes or threatened with a gun or knife?

No ____ If Yes, enter 1 ____

8. Did you live with anyone who was a problem drinker or alcoholic, or who used street drugs?

No ____ If Yes, enter 1 ____

9. Was a household member depressed or mentally ill, or did a household member attempt suicide?

No ____ If Yes, enter 1 ____

10. Did a household member go to prison?

No ____ If Yes, enter 1 ____

Now add up your "Yes" answers: ____
This is your ACE Score.

If you scored more than 4, and as your score increases, the research shows that you are more vulnerable to developing mental and substance use disorders, engage in high-risk sexual behaviors, and more likely to develop diabetes and have heart attacks. This is definitely an indication that you should consult with a mental health professional about the level of care you might need.

Trauma can also occur at any time in life due to exposure to sexual violence, natural disaster, fire, explosion, war, car wreck, assault with a weapon, serious accident, and/or major chronic illness. The toxic stress that results from chronic adversities such as poverty and racism can also lead to traumatic conditions, lessen an individual's ability to manage stressors, and/or compound an individual's experience of other traumas that they endure.

About 20% of people who experience trauma will go on to develop trauma-related disorders—PTSD, depression, and anxiety. Women are particularly vulnerable due to higher incidences of interpersonal violence, such as intimate partner violence and sexual violation. Trauma leaves the brain frozen in time and swimming in fear. The trauma becomes the controlling force in an individual's life whether or not they are aware of it. As discussed in chapter two, trauma impacts how the brain works by increasing levels of circulating stress hormones. These hormones put an individual in the 'flight or fight' zone of survival mode. Some, including myself, have argued that for people with a history of oppression, the "post" in PTSD should perhaps be replaced with "persistent."

If the traumas are horrific and/or occur over a long period and are unresolved, the individual begins to perceive the world as a dangerous place. They can also start feeling incompetent, unable to cope with life's stressors. It is not uncommon for some individuals to self-medicate to avoid these negative feelings and thoughts. Individuals who experience trauma are highly vulnerable to substance use disorders as they turn to drugs to help manage the negative feelings of fear, shame, and/or anger associated with the trauma.

If you question whether or not you are suffering from a traumatic experience in your past, here are some of the ways in which it can show up in your life:

- Feeling trapped in the past
- Narrowing your imagination, play, creativity, mental flexibility, hope, and the ability to envision a bright future
- Making you feel unsafe
- Shaking your trust in Self and others and hampering your intimate relationships
- Feeling a lot of self-blame, guilt and pity
- Ultimately hampering your ability to set goals and carve out an authentic path for your life not based on your earlier suffering

A hallmark of trauma is that we try hard to forget what happened, because at the time the encounter occurred, it was frightening and horrifying. But it is very important to find out if you might be suffering from a traumatic disorder, despite how difficult it might seem to revisit the past. And the good news is that if or when one emotionally processes the fear associated with their trauma, it minimizes its impact on brain functioning, how one processes one's feelings, thoughts and actions, and makes it easier to put the experience in its proper place - the past! This in turn makes it easier to release the fear structure and live more fully in the present.

Even if you don't feel you have experienced any of the situations on the list above, I strongly recommend that if you have ever had any encounters you consider traumatic, you consider taking the three screeners described below.

The first is the screener for PTSD, the Primary Care PTSD Screen for DSM-5 (PC-PTSD-5). This series of questions will ask you if you have had any horrifically stressful/traumatic life experiences, as a result of which: a) you kept reliving/re-experiencing what happened; b) you avoided places and memories of what happened; and, c) you felt aroused, unsafe, jittery, and/or irritable; and, your mood and thoughts about the world became negative.

The second is the screener for depression, the Physician Health Questionnaire (PHQ-9). This screener will ask questions to see if you are currently experiencing depression. These questions will assess whether you have been feeling sad, and/or have lost interest in the things you normally do. It will also ask questions about your appetite, sleep, concentration, and energy level. Most importantly, it will ask if you have feelings of wanting to take your life.

The last screener is for anxiety, the Generalized Anxiety Disorder 7-item Scale (GAD). This screener will ask questions to assess your level of overall anxiety, nervousness, worry, and fear.

If you screen positive for any of these disorders, please see either your primary care provider or a mental health practitioner. This is particularly urgent if you screened greater than four on the ACE scorecard. Treatment for these disorders is quite effective. The first line treatment approach is cognitive behavioral and exposure based talk therapies:

- Prolonged Exposure (PE) utilizes emotional processing techniques to help trauma survivors process their traumatic experiences so as to diminish trauma-related excessive fear and anxiety symptoms
- Cognitive Processing Therapy (CPT) utilizes the process of reframing the negative thoughts about the trauma, especially those that keep one stuck in the negative memory, so as to discover positive ways to manage and learn from the trauma

Another therapeutic modality that has been found effective is Eye Movement Desensitization and Reprocessing (EMDR). EMDR utilizes the process of recalling the trauma while focusing on bilateral sensory input such as back or forth eye movements and hand-tapping. The mechanism of action is unclear, however EMDR has been found to be effective for some individuals.

If you engage in one of these trauma-based therapies and your response is slow or inadequate, your mental health provider may decide to explore medication management as an adjunct to the psychotherapy. The drugs that are indicated and most often used are selective serotonin reuptake inhibitor medications (SSRIs such as Prozac, Zoloft, Paxil Venlafaxine). Be careful about the use of benzodiazepines (e.g. Xanax, Ativan, Klonopin, and Valium) longer than one month, as they can cause physical and/or psychological dependence–addiction. These treatments should definitely be supported with mind-body activities in which breathing is purposive and meditative, such as dance, yoga, tai chi, and capoeira.

The good news is that if you score positive on any of these scales, the treatments discussed earlier are quite effective. What is most important is finding a culturally proficient and well-trained trauma-based mental health clinician with whom you feel safe to self-disclose and self-examine. One of the best ways to determine the fit between you and a potential mental health provider is to make your first visit a consultation, which allows you to not feel any pressure to make a commitment to return. If the energy between you feels right and your gut feelings beckon that this person can relate and empathize with your pain, then by all means return. If that is not so, abort and seek another!

To help break the ice, I will delve further into talk therapy in the next chapter and help to uncover the process.

Screening Tools

PTSD Screener - PC-PTSD-5

Sometimes things happen to people that are unusually or especially frightening, horrible, or traumatic. For example:

• A serious accident or fire
• A physical or sexual assault or abuse
• An earthquake or flood
• A war
• Seeing someone killed or seriously injured
• Having a loved one die through homicide or suicide

Have you ever experienced this kind of event?
   YES   NO

If **no**, screen total = 0 please stop here.
If **yes**, please answer the questions below.

In the past month, have you…

1. Had nightmares about the event(s) or thought about the event(s) when you did not want to?
    YES   NO

2. Tried hard not to think about the event(s) or went out of your way to avoid situations that reminded you of the event(s)?
    YES   NO

3. Been constantly on guard, watchful, or easily startled?
    YES   NO

4. Felt numb or detached from people, activities, or your surroundings?
   YES   NO

5. Felt guilty or unable to stop blaming yourself or others for the event(s) or any problems the event(s) may have caused?
   YES   NO

If you score greater than 3, please see a mental health clinician to confirm whether or not you have PTSD.

Depression Screener - PHQ-9

Over the last two weeks, how often have you been
bothered by any of the following problems?

Keep track of your score:
1. Little interest or pleasure in doing things ___
    Not at all = 0
    Several days =1
    More than half the days = 2
    Nearly every day = 3

2. Feeling down, depressed, or hopeless ___
    Not at all = 0
    Several days =1
    More than half the days = 2
    Nearly every day = 3

3. Trouble falling or staying asleep, or sleeping too
    much ___
    Not at all = 0
    Several days =1
    More than half the days = 2
    Nearly every day = 3

4. Feeling tired or having little energy ___
    Not at all = 0
    Several days =1
    More than half the days = 2
    Nearly every day = 3

5. Poor appetite or overeating ___
    Not at all = 0
    Several days =1

More than half the days = 2
Nearly every day = 3

6. Feeling bad about yourself or that you are a failure or have let yourself or your family down ___
   Not at all = 0
   Several days =1
   More than half the days = 2
   Nearly every day = 3

7. Trouble concentrating on things, such as reading the newspaper or watching television ___
   Not at all = 0
   Several days =1
   More than half the days = 2
   Nearly every day = 3

8. Moving or speaking so slowly that other people could have noticed. Or the opposite: being so fidgety or restless that you have been moving around a lot more than usual ___
   Not at all = 0
   Several days =1
   More than half the days = 2
   Nearly every day = 3

9. Thoughts that you would be better off dead, or of hurting yourself ___
   Not at all = 0
   Several days =1
   More than half the days = 2
   Nearly every day = 3

Now add up your score: ___

The following range is an indication of what your score suggests, but this will be more accurately defined by having a discussion with a professional. Do not hesitate to seek help if you score more than 10. However, seeking a consultation with a professional even if you score in the mild range can also provide benefits.

0-4	Not significant
5-9	Mild depression
10-14	Moderate depression
15-19	Moderately severe depression
20-27	Severe depression

Anxiety Screener - GAD-7

Over the last 2 weeks, how often have you been bothered by the following problems?

1. Feeling nervous, anxious, or on edge ____
   Not at all = 0
   Several days =1
   More than half the days = 2
   Nearly every day = 3

2. Not being able to stop or control worrying ____
   Not at all = 0
   Several days =1
   More than half the days = 2
   Nearly every day = 3

3. Worrying too much about different things ____
   Not at all = 0
   Several days = 1
   More than half the days = 2
   Nearly every day = 3

4. Trouble relaxing ____
   Not at all = 0
   Several days = 1
   More than half the days = 2
   Nearly every day = 3

5. Being so restless that it's hard to sit still ____
   Not at all = 0
   Several days = 1
   More than half the days = 2
   Nearly every day = 3

6. Becoming easily annoyed or irritable ___
    Not at all = 0
    Several days =1
    More than half the days = 2
    Nearly every day = 3

7. Feeling afraid as if something awful might happen ___
    Not at all = 0
    Several days =1
    More than half the days = 2
    Nearly every day = 3

    Now add up your score: ___

The following range is an indication of what your score suggests, but this will be more accurately defined by having a discussion with a professional. Do not hesitate to seek help if you score more than 10. However, seeking a consultation with a professional even if you score in the mild range can also provide benefits.

    5-9   Mild anxiety
    10-14   Moderate anxiety
    >15-19 Severe anxiety

If you scored more than 0 on any of the questions, how difficult have these made it for you to do your work, take care of things at home, or get along with other people?

    Not difficult at all   ___
    Very difficult   ___
    Somewhat difficult   ___
    Extremely difficult   ___

If you have noted that your anxiety has been disabling in your relationships or your ability to function at work or in your community, please seek help from a mental health clinician.

Chapter 9
Taking the Plunge: Talk Therapy

As previously laid out, our individual Self healing work does not erase the influence of the external determinants of mental health, such as social inclusion, freedom from discrimination and violence, and access to economic resources, the lack of which all contribute to deprivation and oppression. Being a part of socially disadvantaged groups, we are more exposed to the risks associated with developing a mental health disorder or problem. As I've discussed in previous chapters, this is an uphill battle for us as a people, being that a climate that respects and protects basic civil, political, socioeconomic and cultural rights is fundamental to mental health promotion.

This compounds the reality that much of life is peppered with disappointment and loss; no one can escape this reality. Whatever the source, external or internal to our being, this can create anxiety and sadness and/or depression. For the most part, therapy can be considered "grief work," the work of letting go of lost dreams, ideals, expectations, places, and/or people; and finding new ways of knitting back together the hole left behind, so as to be whole again in a new way. It is in this spirit that I recommend giving yourself the gift of "talk therapy" facilitated by a competent mental health professional, one with whom you find a good fit.

For many, a safe and trusting therapeutic environment—one that challenges us to go past our comfort zone, but not our safety zone—can help us move toward our dis-ease, lean in, and wade into the memories without being re-harmed by the pain we endured in the past. That is the reason many find tremendous value in talk-therapy for their mental self-care journey. With the ongoing micro- and macro-aggressions Black people face on a daily basis, we can all benefit from having a space wherein we can safely unpack the emotional pain we have had to withstand.

The conditions of people who can benefit from talk therapy are not limited to those in extreme cases. The benefit serves along a continuum of those who are able to function well with lesser degrees of mental health support and just need occasional "tuning up," all the way to those whose disorder/illness creates severe dysfunction and impairment and need a lot of structure and support. Embedded within this range are those who have episodic experiences of being overwhelmed by depression, trauma, and anxiety, those who are suffering from chronic and persistent mental illness, and those with neurotic tendencies who seek adjustment/changes in how they view themselves, others, and the world at large (personality restructuring) so as to optimize their well-being.

As a people, our willingness to access this type of help to journey back to our selves is marred by historical experiences, which have made this benefit unfairly off-limits to our community. It is unfortunate, but understandable, given the medical abuses we have and continue to endure, that seeking mental services is so very maligned and stigmatized in our community. Given that we are exposed disproportionately to the risk of mental suffering, it's even more disturbing that we conversely avoid this proven and sometimes necessary remedy. So many of us suffer unnecessarily on our own due to stigma, economics, or by clinging to survival, when we have so much to gain through talk therapy and have witnessed the damage caused by and to people who need intervention and do not get it.

Talk therapy with a competent, "good enough," mental health therapist makes us feel comfortable in releasing our defensive posturing—that is, becoming vulnerable—and helps us face and break through our resistance to positive change. The competent mental health therapist is one who spends more time listening to and trying to help us understand the connectivity between our thoughts, feelings, unconscious motivations, and actions versus one who is constantly talking and giving advice. Advice giving belongs to coaches and as such is not therapy. This is very important because acceptance and true long-lasting change has to come from within us—it cannot be forced from the outside.

The basic aim of talk-therapies, ranging from cognitive/behavioral to dynamic to analytic, is to help us recognize the unconscious ego defenses we create to protect us from the anxiety that arises when we deal with situations that result from feelings of anger/rage, sadness, fear, disgust, guilt, and shame. Effective therapies help us to push through and beyond the resistance we harbor—which shields us from exposing conflicts related to our unconscious wishes—and brings our fears into our awareness. The aim of such insight is to help us explore and know how these defensive structures became embedded into the distorted schemas we hold about ourselves. For example, "I am not worthy or deserving; I am lesser than; I am ugly; I deserve to be alone," etc. Such insight gives us the ability to make healthier choices. Ultimately, therapy helps us to know the truth about Self, who we truly are.

The negative feelings that go along with our distorted and maladaptive thoughts are usually embedded in our bodies–most commonly our shoulders, neck, chest, throat, and guts. Trauma expert Dr. Besel van der Kolk reminds us that the amygdala, the part of our brain that registers fear, is primitive and does not communicate with our more rational, logical brain during times of stress. This makes it difficult to reasonably talk ourselves out of situations when we are very emotionally aroused. Dr. Van der Kolk further reminds us that our emotions are also stored and registered in the body, which underscores the importance of complementing talk therapy with intentional bodywork. Mind-body integrative work catalyzes the healing process and makes it happen that much more quickly.

There are three important aspects of ourselves that therapy should facilitate our comprehension of:

- How we resist feeling the disturbing emotions that happen in our inner life
- How we unconsciously respond to others we create intimate relationships with in our adult lives, projecting onto them unresolved conflicts with significant caretakers from our childhood–mother / father
- How we oftentimes project onto others that which we resist owning in ourselves, and in so doing, we blame them for our own shortcomings

The more aware we are of the connection between our negative feelings, the resultant thoughts, the embodied feelings, and dysfunctional behaviors, the easier it is to release them from our minds and our bodies. When we do so, we can learn how to reframe our thoughts, manage our emotions, reduce stress in our bodies, and open up the possibility of healthier choices.

Throughout the process, the good enough therapist helps to give language to the things that happened to cause us pain and discomfort—those experiences that many of us have tightly locked away. S/he further helps us understand how to tolerate those memories related to the negative schemas we carry, which are embedded in fear, sadness, anger, and shame. S/he helps us recognize that the present can no longer harm us; that the danger of the past has indeed passed; and that memories are just that— recollections of a past time in our lives, not our present reality. S/he helps us learn how to live in the reality of the present and acquire a sense of feeling in control, able to regulate/manage our emotions. A therapist does so by assuring that we feel emotionally and physically safe, by helping us build self-awareness, and by teaching us how to strengthen our emotional regulation skills.

Does that therapist need to be our same race or our same gender? Even though race/gender matching might make the processes easier, it is not essential. It certainly is helpful when our therapist can relate to our life experience, when they have some firsthand knowledge of the context within which we live our lives. However, what is most important is that the therapist is empathic; that is, can understand how you feel, and as a result create a positive, non-judgmental, trusting, and warm working alliance with you.

Ultimately, the role of the therapist is to release our own capacity for self-reflection and awareness. The good enough therapist recognizes that we are the experts of our lives, and that deep within us is the resolution of our pain and the know-how to lessen our suffering.

The following is a brief summary of work that I did with a client whose fortitude and resilience was amazing. I am humbled to have contributed some to her healing.

Woman Nuh Cry:

WS is a forty plus year old woman whom I saw in therapy 12 years after her four children were killed in an automobile accident. She had not sought therapy before: "I tried to be a super Christian. God helped me to not blow my head off. I needed more though because deep inside I felt helpless and was destroying myself with food. I should have sought therapy earlier. Just as I thought I was okay and had gotten myself together, all my children died."

{Of note, since our captivity and/or colonization, religion/faith has always been an important component of coping with stressors and trauma for many of us. At times, however, the belief in a stress-free, idyllic afterlife is not sufficient to quell our here-and-now pain, as WS eventually learned. In other words, spiritually bypassing her present day mental pain did not bring her the soothing or comfort and relief from her burden. I have heard many Black people say they do not seek therapy because Jesus is their therapist. I have often wondered if a loving and caring higher power would want them to wallow unnecessarily in pain. And I have wondered if perhaps Jesus would not want to guide them to seek care, similar to when/if they have a ruptured appendix. He certainly would want them to seek the services of a surgeon. I am oftentimes left wondering why we think that faith, prayer, and therapy are mutually exclusive.}

Over the past 12 years since their death, WS gained 150 pounds: "I used the food to soothe my pain. My husband and I would eat so much, sitting in bed, just eating and eating. And people fed us constantly in the first year after the accident." She felt disgusted with herself, ashamed of her weight gain and the resultant morbid obesity. WS also developed severe hypertension and arthritis. She was terrified of being in a car accident and running off the road and dying.

She reported that all her life she had been in pain: "my childhood was just trauma and I have no pleasant memories of then." Her father died when she was five years old and her mother died when she was 11 years old. From the ages eight to eleven, WS took care of her ailing mother. Her mother's boyfriend molested her (WS) during that same time period. He died seven months before her mother. She could not understand how her mother did not know what was going on, and why she had not protected her: "Why was nobody checking on me? No one was paying attention to me. No one took the time to make me feel special. I wish I could have confronted my mother before she died." After her mother's death, she went to live with an aunt, who emotionally and verbally abused her.

WS reported being very sexually active during her adolescence: "I was looking to feel loved." As a result, she got pregnant during high school and "it took me 22 years to get back to college." She was involved in abusive relationships with men until she met her current husband, fourteen years older than her, with whom she had two children. She'd had to flee her first husband, who was abusive and with whom she also had two children.

At the beginning of therapy, she reported difficulty sleeping, anxiety, and eating to comfort herself, especially at night. She also reported chronic pain due to her weight. WS was resistant to revisiting the accident. She did not want to speak about what happened and instead brought the newspaper account for me to read. She was terrified of opening up to the pain. She was afraid of processing her true emotions, as a result of which she stayed frozen in her fear and in the past: "How can I be in the present and remain sane with what happened in the past?"

During the course of therapy, WS realized that she did not allow herself to grieve because she was scared she would get depressed and end up wanting to stay in bed all day, doing nothing, and eating even more unhealthily. She was also concerned that being joyful would mean that she was disloyal to the memory of her children. {Of note, I have heard an even more sinister attitude from a colleague who lost her sister to an opioid overdose, "I don't want therapy to do what it should do and help me be okay. I always want to be depressed about her being gone."}

I diagnosed WS with PTSD and Depression. My initial therapeutic work with her consisted of psycho-education about the impact of trauma on her mind and body. I also began the process of slowly and safely confronting/re-exposing her to the pain and suffering of her loss, so that she could begin the deeper process of grief work. My approach was to adopt a comforting and supportive stance, yet gently confront her resistance to and avoidance of dealing with her loss.

Within a few months, her sleep improved, her anxiety became more manageable, and her capacity for introspection and self-awareness significantly improved. She came to realize that she was in the helping profession with children because no one took care of her when she was young. Also, after her own loss, it helped her to feel that she was saving other children. She became determined to try to find some closure, despite knowing that the hole would always be present. Towards the end or our sessions together, she reported being better able to deal with the emptiness and pain of her children's death: "I cannot stay

in locked up, crying and having a pity party with myself."
She realized that she was slowly self-destructing by doing
so.

Attention to her self-care became real. She expressed
being more committed to her fitness program—being
more consistent with her attendance at the gym, and
walking in the park close by. She also adopted a healthier
diet by minimizing junk food and adopting a more plant-
based diet. She also realized that she had memorialized and
ritualized her pain. She stopped using their birthdays as
passwords and stopped using the number four (four
children died) as a symbol of hanging on to them.

With much joy, on her last session, she reported that she
had passed a licensure exam that she had failed twice in
the past. She was proud that she did not celebrate with
food, as she would have done before. And, whereas
insomnia was a burden and a symptom of her distress in
the past: "I was so happy, I could not sleep last night!"

She did express some anxiety about ending our sessions
together, but wanted to try standing on her own and
focusing on her most pressing issue—that of losing the
weight she had gained. Like WS, when therapy terminates
for many individuals with whom I have worked, they leave
feeling much lighter and more capable of handling the
stressors that are bound to turn up in their lives. Usually,
mild separation anxiety will emerge, along with the return
of some of the symptoms they first came to therapy to
address. The work then is to remind them that they have
new tools they learned in therapy: new self-awareness that
will allow them, on their own, to continue the process of
mentalizing, self-examination, and more authentic

decision-making.

For me, therapy is not complete until I have helped my patients think more deeply about all or some of those concerns about our existence as human beings which none of us can escape. So after I have facilitated their journey of taking off the masks and releasing the skeletons in their personal biography, I always try to end with two to three sessions on coming to terms with those existential issues, to further decrease their anxiety about living. Hence, with WS, we also spent time exploring her philosophical ideas about the meaning of life and death. Her understanding and deliberations were based in Christian teaching.

These core universal existential realities arise as part of the human experience wherein we seek meaning and purpose to our lives, while at the same time we are confronted with the realities of isolation, freedom, and death. I encourage you to ponder the following existential questions:

- *What Am I?* Are you curious about the reason for our existence—what is the point of our life? Do you search for meaning and purpose in your life—Why am I here? What am I here to do? What am I passionate about doing?
- *Do I fall in love or stand in love?* Do you fear loneliness or do you cling and try to fuse with others? Are you aware of your isolation/aloneness, in spite of your desire for connection and belonging? Do you think about the reality that we can never fully share our consciousness with another—that we are all separate beings and cannot get past another's skin? Therefore, how do you turn up in the interpersonal realm?
- *How have I chosen to live within the mystery and map out my journey through life?* How do you pursue the groundless-ness of your potential freedom within the bondage of

dependence on others in creating your life experiences? To the extent that we all live in a universe without any sign posts or any inherent design, and are the architect/author of our playbook—our choices and actions, how do you compile your life?

- *How do I live in each moment? How do I want to depart?* Carlos Castenada declared that death is always on, traveling along with us on our left shoulder. An undeniable reality is that our death is certain, but the time it will occur is uncertain. Hence, how aware are you of your primal wish to continue to live and persist in your own being in spite of the inevitability of your death?

In exploring these universal life issues, uncertainty, curiosity, questioning, wonderment, and doubt are our best friends. Age-old wisdom teaches us that life's journey offers no certitude, no guaranteed roadmap. Holding onto the rigidity and dogma of handed down belief systems can lead to oscillation from one emotional pole to the other, creating instability in how we experience life. When we let go, we come to find out that it is so much less jarring to hang out in the grey zone of life.

But for Black lives, our existence is peppered with another reality that nuances our understanding of these issues. Having to always confront the social construct of race and the resultant debasement of Black life by the diabolical hegemony of white supremacy, we must grapple with what it means to be free. Throughout our history, beginning with the actions of Black maroons and all other freedom fighters then and now, our affiliation with marginalized Indigenous peoples and our ponderings in various art forms—music, literature, and dance—we have been in the struggle for Black liberation to be seen. Ralph Ellison summed it up best in his seminal work, *The Invisible Man,* "I am a man of substance, of flesh and bone, fiber and liquids—and I might even be said to possess a brain. I am invisible, understand, simply because people refuse to see me." We must continue the struggle to assert the right to be seen in our full humanity and presence, to affirm to our Self and others that Black life matters.

Frantz Fanon suggested however that we have to claim responsibility for the humanity of "I" if indeed one is going to break the chains and heal the wounds of racism: "I am not the slave of the Slavery that dehumanized my ancestors...I am my own foundation." Similarly, Bob Marley reminded us that only we "can rid our Self of mental slavery" and heal our mind.

CHAPTER 10

Contemplative Practices

When I discover who I am, I will be free.
~ Ralph Ellison

How do we fully engage in the processes of liberating our minds? In addition to uncovering the sources of our grief and discomforts and learning more adaptive ways of feeling and thinking, contemplative practices can help us solidify our mental foundation for the healing work to continue. Uncovering, as occurs in the more standard Western therapeutic processes, helps us gain insight into the source of conflicts and the ways in which we have managed them. Adding Eastern-derived contemplative practices to deepen our self-awareness helps us better witness and understand how our mind works in the present moment.

In other words, the other important component of the healing process is noticing and deepening our awareness of how our inner Self and outer reality coexist in the present moment. Inner-focused and concentration meditation; open awareness mindfulness (sensory awareness and presence); visualization; and/or affirming prayer in which we are listening and not talking to the universe are all contemplative practices that assist us in witnessing and awakening to the reality of our Self and the world as is, without judgment or desire. They give us space to ponder whether they are in harmony or if they contradict.

These processes also allow us to better observe and understand the illusions and delusions our minds create to avoid the uncomfortable realities of our present existence. With devotion to these practices we become more aware of how to neutralize and liberate our Self from being governed by our mind's distortion of what really is. We no longer need to be protected from the rough spots of life as they unfold because we have established the mental resilience to accept and move beyond them.

Additionally, pain functions to alert us to injury, harm, hurt, or damage in our being. To that end, pain is necessary for our survival. The painful reality that occurs as we encounter the disappointment/shock/loss that comes naturally from being alive can initially create suffering. On-going suffering, however, comes from our mind's catastrophizing and projection into the future, or back into the past, manifested by "what ifs," "should haves," and "would haves." Eventually, as we fully accept the reality of things as they really are and accept the impermanence and transitory nature of all things without clinging to how we wish things would be, pain will not morph into suffering. Instead, by staying open to the ebb and flow of pain and joy, we are bolstered by the awareness that most times we will rise again.

When we engage in contemplative practices, the aim is not solely to try to stop thinking and enter into blissful nirvana or "the taste of enlightenment." These practices can directly help us awaken—"get woke," become more aware of our senses, and live in the now. They help us to listen to the messages from inside and out, rather than simply talking through our wants and needs. They also allow us to explore areas of unhealthy habits and addictions that might plague us because contemplative processes give us enough distance between a stimulus and the set of automatic, default thoughts and/or actions to which we usually respond. We get more freedom to make choices that reflect better long-term consequences of our actions, rather than short-term pleasure and gratification.

Being able to create solitude and quietude is a prerequisite, whether we contemplate in stillness or motion, in communion or retreat. The easiest and most effective path to quieting our mind in order that we might witness and notice is to focus on our breath— experience our breathing. Slow and deep abdominal breaths expand our chests and activate our vagus nerve. This nerve is the longest nerve in our bodies. It wanders from our brain, through our neck, chest, and abdomen. One of its major functions is to activate our parasympathetic nervous system, making it the antidote to our stress-related sympathetic "fight or flight" nervous system. When activated, it brings us calm.

As stated earlier, there are many different types of contemplative practices and multiple pathways to creating inner peace. We might engage in mindfulness practices in which the attention is focused outwards on gaining clarity of that which we are sensing in our universe, that which we see, what we hear, what we smell, what we feel to the touch, that which we taste, in the true reality of the present moment. By increasing our present moment awareness, we escape the tendency to wallow in past hurts or future worries. By being more mindful of our bodily sensations, feelings, and thoughts, we increase our awareness of how we interact with others, our external world, and ourselves.

Another option is to engage in more inward focused meditation, wherein we are observing our thoughts and seeing our Self without judgment. This allows us to begin to liberate our mind, detach from, and transcend our sorrows. In this style of meditation, we go beyond our thinking and begin to journey from the embittered/painful state of mind to a more enlightened, perfect space of light and true knowing. And as the song told us, when we free our mind, the rest follows. This type of meditation can take us into deep silence, in which we experience deep time not bounded by chronology, where we can suspend beliefs and experience things as they truly are.

We can also engage in loving kindness meditation wherein we send loving kindness to ourselves and/or others. Loving kindness directed toward our Self helps us discover and feel the sacredness of who we truly are and to let go of the false constructs that our ego uses to distract us from that reality.

Yet another contemplative method is to engage in affirming visualization and contemplation of the more positive states of our being:

- How can I love others and myself more deeply?
- How can I reclaim my inner beauty—come home to the grace and depth of who I am?
- How can I continue to soften and open my heart?
- How can I lessen being a victim of time—how can I mitigate stress by yielding to the gift of being present with time, not fighting it?
- How does my soul, my true Self, connect to the divine creation?
- How can I forgive others and myself and not linger in anger and envy?
- How can I be the author of my biography and create my true plot through life?
- How do I come to value myself?

The journey toward the attainment of a more transcendent and enlightened state is forever ongoing. Sometimes spiraling up, at other times spiraling down. We are bound to bump upon unexplainable and unpredictable loss, disappearance, and removal as we move hither and thither along our path. There is no smooth sailing into nirvana. Oftentimes just when we think we made it to the finish line and put final closure to a painful chapter of grief, the pain resurfaces. Full relief was but an illusion. This can be an indication that we did not fully pull back all the energy connected to longing for the objects/persons that we lost, and which contributed to our suffering. And so we have to start over again, hopefully a little further along the path, but this time letting go a bit more.

This poem by Rilke speaks to the process of ending suffering and finding resilience that we all seek. And what is personal resilience? It is the ability to resist, absorb, accommodate to, transform, and/or recover when facing life's challenges. In other words, the ability to bounce back, build one's Self back better, and spring forward into new opportunities.

Part Two, Sonnet XXIX by Rainer Maria Rilke

Quiet friend who has come so far,
feel how your breathing makes more space around you.
Let this darkness be a bell tower
and you the bell. As you ring,
what batters you becomes your strength.
Move back and forth into the change.
What is it like, such intensity of pain?
If the drink is bitter, turn yourself to wine.

In this uncontainable night,
be the mystery at the crossroads of your senses,
the meaning discovered there.

And if the world has ceased to hear you,

say to the silent earth: I flow.
To the rushing water, speak: I am.

Some questions to Self:
- *Do I give myself increasing moments each day to be fully alive with all senses, so as to witness the realities that exist inside and outside of me?*
- *Do I know who is in the mirror?*

We are doing time from birth to death. Change and suffering are inevitable along the course. At some point we will all experience hurt, disappointment, disillusionment, and harm. Buddhist philosophy teaches that life's constants are change and experiences that can create suffering. However, by letting go of delusions (false beliefs) and instead dealing with reality as it unfolds, we can move through the suffering and liberate our Self, rather than getting stuck in it. We can accept life's changes, challenges, and obstacles and find freedom. We all have a choice: do we get stuck in our hurt, or do we ride the wave until we can release it, through deeper understanding of its cause, thus discovering the lesson our hurt is trying to teach us? Through contemplative practices we can observe our Self and create the distance necessary to learn how to better self-regulate and decrease the impact of potential suffering. To paraphrase Mary J. Blige, contemplative practices can bring us to a state of "no more sufferation."

Chapter 11

Black Mind Redemption - Imagining a Higher Self

Allowing our minds to get still and roam free in imagination land is the primer to achieving the healing and inner self-navigation we seek. The companion to imagination is visualization—seeing that which we seek. If indeed you seek freedom from the chains that bind us to captivity, if you want to move closer to our divine Self, I invite you to take this imaginal journey with me. I invite you to let go of an Afro-enslaved past that has been peppered with inhumane and brutal patriarchal evil. Instead, radically imagine an Afro-future graced with the feminine empress, the universal Yin, the source of a loving mother divine. Everyone benefits from free, mindful exploration. Even a most revered scientist gave voice to its value:

"I am enough of the artist to draw freely upon my imagination. Imagination is more important than knowledge. Knowledge is limited. Imagination encircles the world."-Albert Einstein, Saturday Evening Post, October 26, 1929.

And once again, as was made clear by the Prophet Robert Nesta Marley, channeling the voice of the Almighty, we have to free ourselves from mental slavery for only we can set free our minds. Imagination allows for transformation and transcendence. How better than to imagine, visualize, and dream a metaphorical journey toward freedom!

After each of the following stations, take a few minutes to allow your own creative dreamscape, whether in writing or drawing, to imagine your own journey in that space and place.

Station 1 - In the Beginning

Imagine:

It is a dark and dreary night as you begin your journey into
imagined flight.
There are no stars smiling warm and bright
Thunderous hisses and lightening kisses serve as your only
guide

You seek shelter in the abandoned barn
The storm is steadily worsening and bellowing messages of
possible harm.
You feel so very weary and forlorn.

You lie down in a forsaken manger that is as unyielding as
Eve's unpardonable sentence

Still haunted by your dreams of emptiness
You drift into restless loneliness.

You listen to the wails coming from beside your head as
you lay on the pillow of lead,
Behold, a veiled woman is crouched at your bed.

You want to get to know her—Her age? The color of her
skin? Her dress? Her hair how long? Are there shoes on
her feet?
Her wretched form is so familiar

You rise and kneel beside her as she speaks the psalms of
the downtrodden
She turns her head, embarrassed that you will see that her
soul is almost dead.

Her eyes are closed, frozen in fright; she cannot see that
she is standing in the shadow of her light

Meet your Slave Lady
Hush her tales and hold her hand
Whisper softly in her ear:
Come journey with me
Inward to your sleeping soul
And outer to the universe
As you journey with me to the promised land.

Station 2 – Dawn

Imagine:

It is long past midnight
Morn is preparing to be reborn
Dawn gently kisses your sleeping head,
Inviting you to join her mystery function
Held daily in her court at the Rainbow junction
You escape sleep's hard cold bosom and
Crawl away from her arms, into the night owl's last bawl

You waltz through a garden of morning glory
Filled with red roses, orange mums, yellow daises, green
pansies, blue lilies, purple freesias, white gardenias
You inhale the fragrant blooms and
Sip the brew of the pure morning dew

You groove to the flutes of the angels
Surely your cup runneth over with music

Intoxicated, you suspend all thoughts and place then next
to your heart

You delve into the still darkness
Drifting, drifting
Feeling light as a lark
Deeper and deeper
You sink into blissful reverie
To the rhapsody of time immortal

You hear a trumpet sound high above from the heavenly
mound
Your timeless spell still unbroken

147

You see the chariots bursting forth upon the horizon
Drawn by cherubs swathed in sparkling red
The velvet curtains begin to open as the music goes dead, and
Slowly, silently, the sun lifts her golden head
Striding triumphantly, spraying kisses from red-painted lips

You linger in her majestic grip and
Chant her wondrous praise
You scream out loud to the virgin sky
I too have come alive

Station 3 – The Valley of the Shadow of Life

Imagine:

It is mid-morn
Reluctant you leave Eden
Continue you must the search for deliverance
Goodbye to self-pity and wretched penance

A bevy of whizzing bees close by suck you into their bumbling high
You flit with them through a pregnant valley
Bursting alive with red flowers and trees

The brightly colored butterflies frolicking alongside
Pluck petals and throw them at your feet
"Queen for a day", your royal carpet greets
"Your highness," a nearby stream gurgles, "let me rub those tired feet with rocks smooth as polished beads."

Then next, orange-bellied fish-in-waiting, eager and ready to mingle
Strum tunes on your battered soles that make you tingle
You succumb to your leisure, exploding as you surrender to the pleasure

Red-bellied birds hovering above whistle you come rest in their forest alcove
You heed their knowing cry and follow them to their haven away from mother sky

You lie beneath a Poinciana tree, blossoms flaming like the Red Sea
You claim the giant roots as anchor, the fallen leaves your cover

You drift into nature's girth, and take your place on top of
mother earth

Your awareness extends outward to the branches end.
You breathe deeply and slowly, as
You inhale nature's calm and exhale your worries
You loosen the hold of your muscles held tight, and
Let them gradually release their rigid fight
You sink deep into your floating body, spirit soaring, soul
ascending
You find the space between the breaths where nothing
exists but Self eternal
Boundaries dissolved, you fall into the belly of the earth
Swallowed up
You become one with all

Station 4 – Fire Dance

Imagine:

It is high noon
The sun is so fierce
No pore has escaped her pierce
Amidst her centered radiance she erases your shadow
Spinning you into a trance
Spellbound
You begin your sacred dance

You leave the royal forest and head towards the foothills
Where the hollow lake welcomes your body's bake

Her mermaid welcomes you with arms outstretched
Your scorching soul succumbs to her erotic hold
And you enter and swim through her every fold

Quenched,
You prance through the nearby orange meadow
Ablaze with mushrooming sunflowers

You join the sun-drenched crickets preparing for midday
bacchanal
"Creatures of pleasure" is their call:
The drum beats
Your heart leaps
Faster and faster
Louder and louder
Hotter and hotter
Wilder and wilder...

Neon fireflies charge the air with desire
Your soul once ice is now on fire

You sip the sweet warm nectar freshly spun by Queen Bee
You savor the liquid jubilee
You whirl in bliss aglow with ecstasy, and
Become the music, the dance electric
From your head to your shoulders
Down your arms to your feet

You pulsate in the stillness
Close to orgasmic
You reclaim your soul creative

Station 5 – The Healing Waters

Imagine:

It is mid-afternoon
The sun so hot and high in her terrain
How you desperately wish it would rain

You journey down the rugged mountain to the sea, and
Let the flowing waters wash away your useless ego and pride
In and out, up and down, round and about
Left bare, with nothing left to hide

You rest by the cliff smoking thunder down the waterfall
Bared naked, you let the sun's warm, yellow hue
Blanket you from the piercing wind
Seemingly trying to color you blue

You let the waves' quiet thunder rise up and rock you
You ride their never-ending reel, and
Let them erode the last few layers of your tightly wrapped
peel
Spiraling down to the core
Your soul is made bare, trapped no more

You lift off and soar to the ones whose hurt is the hardest
to endure
You bid them come close so that they can hear
How they have caused you so much sorrow and fear

You listen as they tell of their living hell
Feeling like Judas, the disciple fell

Lighter in truth

You float to the one whom you have brought the most
sorrow
You cannot let it wait for another tomorrow
You listen as they tell their story so blue
How starting from love and trust
Everything plummeted into sadness and fuss

You say sorry for all the pain and worry
Face-to-face in loving embrace
You wash away each other's bitter tears
Ones that previously stung sharper than mace

Together, you exchange solemn vows of repentance

Station 6 – The Sea of Love

Imagine:

It is late afternoon

The sea, now resting quietly beneath her turquoise sheet
Beckons you come take refuge from the still glaring heat

You embrace the comfort of her womb so mighty
And wrap your soul in her soothing arms, ever so tightly
You immerse your head next to her beating heart, just so lightly
You sink into the waves of her thick love nectar

You wash ashore on an isle of effervescent green
The most enchanting beauty your eyes have ever seen.
Shipwrecked maybe, but ready for adventure
Barefoot and carefree you skip through fields of myrtle trees swaying in the breeze
Their whistling tunes melt the freeze of your loves unrequited, hearts never united
Unfettered, you watch as the heartaches become unleashed.
You pass through an iridescent archway, sparkling with emerald fern
Behold the sacred Goddess appears
Suspended upon a translucent throne, lavishly draped in a jeweled sheath
Tantalized, her aura pulls you closer into the promise of her merciful caress

You fall to your knees and kiss her holy feet

She beckons you come close and share her seat

You move closer into her tender embrace
While she wipes the endless tears flowing from your face
She feeds you berries from her golden bowl,
Ending the years of famine starving your soul

She adorns you in a regal garb,
Satin studded with sapphires, opals, and pearls
She crowns you with diamonds ablaze and on fire

You yield to her charm and grace
Absorbing the divine beauty streaming on your face

You emerge buoyant with love and humility

Station 7 – Songs Up High

Imagine:

Evening has settled on your island paradise
Dusk invites you to attend her last picture show of the day
Held nightly at the court high above Blue River Bay

The sky, dressed in her royal blue silk robes
Has offered her stage to the vanishing light
Giving birth to the dark mysterious night

Jubilantly, you climb to the top of the hill
And take front row for the celebration,
The premier top bill for time ever changing, never still

You hear the trumpets sound the mighty archangels' lure,
Heralding their golden chariots come once more
To take their sun way up high to his other home across the
sky
Triumphantly he takes one last bow, spraying final good-
bye kisses
From lips still slightly red, faintly painted now

You applaud the celestial spectacle
The cherub in-waiting, swathed in lively blue shrouds,
Lay his head upon the puffy white clouds
They cover him with the warm blue sky, his blanket
Majestic he lays in his cradle
You throw him one last parting kiss from your bluff side
seat
Slowly he shuts his weary eyes as the birds chant their
sacred lullaby

The curtains begin to close

You open your eyes to the voice of the sages echoing in
the river below
And let their sacred sounds vibrate in you

Life begins in me
Life maintains in me
Life ends in me
Life is me

Station 8 – Crystal Temple By The River

Imagine:

It is the magic moment, twilight
Sister stars are smiling bright
Mother moon is glowing ripe
Beaming light kisses upon the night
A night fairy on an enchanted boat hovering by
Offers you safe passage to her secret shrine
"I've come to take you mine, my forever valentine, my sweet concubine"
Unable to feign the slightest chagrin
You slip into her sumptuous mystique
Assuming the opulence of her sensuous physique

Together you wind your way up the River Blue
Beneath the amethyst sky giving faint light to your view

You stop by the crystal temple along her banks and step ashore
Sprinkling libations and offering thanks
To those gone before to prepare the place
Where you will eventually step out in grace

You enter and lie at the purple altar
Vestal maidens ever so pure and chaste
With golden chains draping tie waist
Remove your dusty worn-out clothes
And massage you all over with sandalwood

You inhale the sweet violas' essence, mixed with burning frankincense
They swathe you in purple silk and feed you honey sweetened milk

Crowning you with garlands, they proclaim you grand high
priestess

You anoint their heads with lavender oil and rub them all
over with myrrh, so pure
You mix their bloody flow with lilacs, offering for the
waiting earth

You chant up high to the Goddess of fertile splendor
Bless us the bearer of
The eternal fruits of life
Open up all our senses
To then, now and forever

Station 9 – Soul Flight

Imagine:

Midnight has come to your temple of gold
It is time to rest your weary souls
Surrender you must, at last and heed the angel's thrust

You drift into blissful sleep, silvery white narcissus as pillow
Your soul once full, now light as feathery willow

Suddenly your dreams are pierced with a vibrant kiss
You awaken to the Moon Goddess
Calling out to you, her newly found Sis
"Come visit in my garden
Eve has claimed her pardon
Eden can now be retaken."

She leads you to a gazebo laden with fragrant vines

You sip the nectar of honey suckle, wine of the divine
You lather in the juice of the sweet night jasmine
And wrap your soul in the warm, soft light
Slipping deep into the night
Your body begins to float aside
You glide naked into liquid flight
You ascend higher and higher into the magic chute
As the owls serenade you with their silver flutes
You hop upon a silver moonbeam spiraling in her sacred stream
Spinning faster than light
You enter the land beyond the night

All of Self becomes alight

All pathways of being become bright
Duality merges as opposites unite
Kaleidoscope of ageless visions move forward and
backward into one
Timeless and space-less you meet the sky
Your slave lady rejoins her liberty
Dark and light together in unity

You claim yourself Eternal

Chapter 12

Physical Self-Care

Our physical body is the vessel through which we experience being alive. It is the foundation of our being. When it stops functioning, we exist no more in the form in which we are now experiencing ourselves. We die. Simultaneous with paying attention to and minding our mind, i.e. mentalizing, it is incumbent upon us to attend to the maintenance of our body and how it might have been harmed, directly or indirectly, by the language of our hearts—our painful emotions.

Our body holds the memory of our pain and fears, even when our mind is trying to forget. Recall this being exampled earlier, through the findings of the ACE study, which showed that having four or more adverse childhood experiences leads to a two-fold increased risk of severe obesity. Recall the rapid beating of our heart or the queasiness in our stomachs when we are frightened. Or the sense of lightheadedness we might feel when we are overcome with joy.

When we embody our pain, mindful and purposeful movements that are in harmony with our breath can help us to relearn how to inhabit and own our whole being. In gaining agency over our body, we build confidence in our total Self, which lays the groundwork for seeing our true inner beauty and worth. Yoga, drumming, capoeira, singing, and marital arts are practices that can help us befriend and recreate safety in our bodies. They are conduits through which we connect to our body and mind in healthier ways.

We must also be particularly careful about what we put into our body to fuel it—that which we eat. As much as is possible, we should try to eat more plant-based, wholesome, organic foods and avoid animal-based foods and those with preservatives. What we eat or not can either be a source of healing or a contributor to or source of disease. Similarly, we should pay attention to the air we breathe. To whatever extent we can, we should avoid living in areas with poor air quality or that bring smoke or carcinogens into our lungs. Our gastrointestinal tract and lungs are the portals between our body and the outer world. We want our intake to be as clean and healthy as possible. We should never forget that it is the mind, together with our Qi, that animates our experience of being alive in our physical bodies.

We must find creative ways of routinizing our practice of moving our bodies so that they do not become weighed down by inertia. Recall the beauty of our bodies moving through space—from the fast moving body of Usain Bolt running the 200 hundred meter to the collective precision of synchronized dance movements of the Alvin Ailey Dance Company. We must develop a physical fitness program that will keep our bodies well oiled—be it frequent walking, jogging, running, biking, or dancing.

As we nurture our physical insides, we must also provide self-care to the outside of our physical being. Falling in love with the shell we are in is a healthy and important vanity. Owning the journey to a healthier Self, truly loving, caressing, and pampering our body can be a difficult one, especially for Black women. The look of our Black bodies has been the object of denigration and shaming for so long. One or more of these confrontations about our physical looks may ring true to you:

- Our families checking the color of our ears when we were first born
- Not being chosen for lead parts in school plays because they were reserved for white girls of European descent or European appearing Black girls
- Being the objects of unwanted sexual acts
- Being told that because we were Black, we were ugly: "if you are Black, step back"
- Being passed over romantically for those with lighter hue
- Being told that only multi-racial need apply
- Being told that we are the least desirable in the on-line dating world
- Being told that a horse is more desirable than an image of us being put on a magazine cover
- Being told that even though we just won Olympic gold, our kinky-coiled hair does not look "good" enough
- Being forced to assign curl patterns to our hair
- Thinking that sewing/weaving/gluing/putting other people's non-kinky hair on our heads makes us more desirable

Dr. Nadia Ellis, Professor of English at USC Berkely, had the following to say about Black women's acculturation regarding our sense of beauty ideals:

The ways in which normative notions of what's pretty are outside of us and then we take them in and we take them on and we put them on and then they come inside. It's fascinating how powerful the aesthetic seems to be for

Black women. It's true for all women and girls that there's some notion that we are having to attend to ourselves always, and that we are having to speak about our self-presentation in ways that are just not…the pressures are not the same for boys. But it feels to me true that the idea of the aesthetic or the category of beauty has a certain kind of pressure for Black girls, or for non-white girls, because we've often felt excluded from the category. And so I think that we can be very playful with it—sometimes earnest, sometimes erotic, sometimes ironic, sometimes distanced. The fact that always seems to be there is the way in which we always have to have some relationship to beauty and make-up and the spectacle of self-presentation. I find that very tiring. It's just yet another style of socialization that we have to master and I think we're often judged on how well we're mastering it.

I remember, growing up as a girl, being a tomboy, being inattentive to normative ideas of femininity and having people check me on that. Sometimes with love, I had aunts who loved me and I think wanted me to fit in in a particular kind of way, so they would give me dresses and tell me to comb my hair in a certain kind of way. To this day I still actually have some trauma around that, even though I now understand that it was coming from love. How I experienced this, when I was a child, was that there was something wrong with the way that I looked and that I could just never meet the standard. It didn't matter; there was always something wrong with me. And I felt like there was more attention paid in any number of settings to what I looked like than there was to anything else about me, so it wasn't about what I was thinking about or what I read or how rambunctious I was or what sports I might be interested in. I just felt like none of that registered because what was always front and center was my physical appearance. And unsurprisingly, what that did was that it made me overly self-conscious about my appearance and therefore made me not want to feel embodied. So it had the opposite effect than what maybe loving people may have wanted from me, which is that they wanted me to feel like I could flourish in my body. But I think too much attention to it just makes me feel like it's a problem that you want to get rid of. So that's an ongoing journey for me, figuring out how to have a certain kind of acceptance of my body and then also a kind of lightness around the aesthetics because it feels like there's been always so much pressure.

One of the things I've been thinking about a lot with Black girls is how much, even though there's all this pressure about how we look and all these expectations around being stylish, there's also a way in which we are not allowed to be thought of as delicate or vulnerable. I loved being strong, from the time I was really tiny, I just had this idea that I wanted to have muscles, muscles really attracted me and felt like an ideal I wanted to strive for. I wanted to be tough. But I also feel like not every girl wants to be tough, not every Black girl wants to be tough. And whether or not you want it, I think it's imposed upon you. There's this notion that you can't be weak and that you have to persist.

Dr. Ellis gives narrative to the reality that for many Black women, our own beauty and worth is based on how we measure up to other ideals non-mirroring of our self-identity and our phenotype. Feminized European looks are the gold standard upon which Black women's beauty is judged—the color of our skin, the size of our nose, and the texture of our hair. Especially when it comes to our hair! For many, we are still tangled up in the negative narratives that have been weaved about our "good" or "bad" hair.

Therefore, for many Black women, our freedom, our healing is locked in our hair. Healing from these collective racialized traumas that populate Black norms and belief systems is imperative. We must get past the shaming and honor the divine beauty bestowed upon us by the Creator. We have to look in the mirror, welcome and affirm our external glamour as well as our inner grace. As was so nobly stated by Kahlil Gibran:

Beauty is life when life unveils her holy face
But you are life and you are the veil
Beauty is eternity gazing at itself in a mirror
But you are eternity and you are the mirror.

We must also remember that we are descendants of the continent where life began. May we remember the "Songs of Solomon" to the beautiful Queen Makeda, the Queen of Sheba of Ethiopia:

You are beautiful my love. Your eyes look out, gentle, through your veil, your hair fleeces down, thick and rich as a whole flock of goats streaming down Mt. Gilead.

Did the sun just rise? Who is this just came in, dawn-clad, sun lovely and moon bright, amazing, radiant, frighteningly beautiful. Your head is majestic as Mt. Carmel, your hair heavy, thick as royal purple cloth, indeed a king has already been caught in your curls.

It may be easy to agree that our physical body is the vessel through which we experience being alive. But we might truly need to interrogate whether we are fully present in our bodies and if we live embodied in our sacred physical being. Do we truly honor and nurture our bodies? Whether large efforts or small meaningful steps, what more could we be doing to help our physical being thrive? Some of the rituals and practices in the next chapter may help lay the foundation for an improved nurturing relationship with our physical being.

Chapter 13

Healing Practices and Rituals

In our journey to health, we must keep the garden of our mind tilled. And doing so requires cultivating mental hygiene. The following are rituals and practices that can help with that tilling. They focus on actions we can take to work on the ways in which we engage with ourselves or others that may be holding us back and contributing to our woundedness. Not all this will apply to you. And some may have significance only for a phase, while others you may want to adapt as a long-term practice or ritual. On this journey of being mindful of what ails you, so too will you make decisions on what can support your personal healing.

Journaling

Writing/journaling can serve as a helpful tool, especially early in the healing process. Writing down the words that capture how we feel and think gives us momentary reprieve from our ego, which always vigilantly polices our consciousness. The ego functions primarily to defend against having to directly face the anxiety that occurs when our needs are not met or our reality seems too painful. During our childhood years we are totally dependent on others to make our world safe. When they fall short a strong ego helps deflect our pain by distorting reality to a bearable quotient. But as we mature and are no longer as dependent on others to navigate our world, we have to face our reality, as painful as it might seem in the moment. Acknowledging the reality underlying our pain is the first step in being able to discharge the hurt that unresolved wounds wreak on our minds and bodies. The letter below is such an example:

Dear X,

Recently I was privileged to enter a space wherein I felt trusted, comforted, loved, and supported. From this group of beautiful Black women, I unexpectedly drew the strength to say aloud my deepest darkest secret. I write this letter because what transpired between us has had an incredible hold on me. It has inhibited the growth of my relationships. It has prompted me to question my good-ness and my value. It has made me feel unworthy and dishonest. If I continue suppressing the way in which our extremely inappropriate interaction impacted me and the residual damage it caused, I fear I will never give all of myself to another. And I so desperately want to allow someone to love my entire being the way I feel I love others.

The night we crossed the line, with you at the helm slowly leading me into an experience that I knew was wrong, was the culmination of over a year of you flirting and courting me. You have made me feel special and loved and beauti-ful since I was a small child. You were always my favorite charismatic uncle and I sought your attention, love, affection and approval at every impasse. Something changed at some point though. What was once a loving uncle's affectionate gaze turned into leering eyes traveling up and down my blossoming curves, taking in my glowing tan skin. I felt your sharp blue eyes exotifying me in the same way I'd heard you talk about your other brown-bodied conquests. You broke me and I didn't know how to make me whole again.

I will no longer feel unworthy. No more will I devalue myself, failing to share the beautiful gifts I have to give this world. You are a trigger. Your presence in my life continues to harm, traumatize, and shame me. I have to understand and accept that what you value about me is my body and how you've been able to use it as a tool for your own pleasure. You are completely oblivious to my inner beauty. I am intelligent and kind and loving and witty and creative and a host of other things. You don't see it. You don't care. You don't love me. And I refuse to have you in my life. We share the same last name, but from this moment on, we share nothing more.

Sincerely,

Penning a letter like this is just the beginning—the tip of the iceberg; the starting point in the arduous task of peeling back the first layer of the onion's skin—the first whiff of the burn—the opening crack. Once we recognize that our mind, body, and/or spirit are broken and hurting as this letter reveals, the next step should be an introspective therapeutic pathway, as earlier discussed. It is important to understand how pain is manifesting in dysfunctional patterns of woundedness in our body, mind, and spirit. The process of introspection, of going in and searching inwards, increases our conscious awareness of how our feelings, especially the negative ones—sadness, fear, shame, disgust, and anger—influence our thoughts and behaviors and, as a result, impact how we perceive our Self and others, as well as how we turn up in the world around us.

For example, after the release gained by putting words to her pain, the author of the earlier letter followed up with a second to herself, not the villain, moving her closer to realizing that she had the power to change directions and make choices towards a healthier Self. This letter signals the potential for a deeper journey toward the hope of restoring the goodness inherent in her being:

I give myself permission to continue ascending into "adulthood" no matter how scary or daunting. From this moment, I choose to celebrate responsibility and authority and autonomy. I release myself from anxiety caused by fear of becoming an adult and doing so alone. I will bravely become a decision-maker and committed partner. I will carry these titles proudly and with grace, no longer attaching to them guilt or embarrassment of not fulfilling others' expectations of me for traveling a road perhaps less trodden. I will no longer attach my happiness to what I've been told success should look like—that I should be married to a successful man and have children and dress differently and bear no tattoos.

I give myself permission to own my many beautiful identities and stop allowing fear of judgment or loss direct which spaces I occupy and with what level of confidence. I have dated men, but I am queer enough. My father is white, but I am Black enough. I have an office with a window, but I am radical enough. I give myself permission to not only be a queer, Black feminist, but to also una-bashedly adorn myself with these jewels outside of the safety of my own internal dialogue.

I give myself permission to be honest with myself and open up to others; to be willing to reopen past trauma so that I may begin healing myself and engage in my own life more fully. I will confront my father about his alcoholism and drug addiction and the ways it impacted me, without feeling guilty that he may feel guilt or that its been too long and it would be unkind to force him to talk about it. I joke about being a drinker with friends and colleagues alike, but I am terrified of my own potential addiction and how it may ruin my life.

I will admit that being pressured by my uncle to have sex was not okay; that even though I was 18, I was manipulated and it was abuse. I have carried this weight alone for so many years, feeling ashamed and dirty and responsible. How can I tell anyone this? How can I tell my mother? How can I tell my Dad what his half-brother did? What would happen to our family? How can anyone love me when I am so damaged? Who will accept this? How could a partner still find me worthy of their affection knowing of this tabooed incident? I don't know. But I will start by confiding at least a little more in the people I trust most and stop lying about the cause of the self-inflicted scars on my body.

I give myself permission to stop comparing my struggles against those of others and silencing myself because I deem my own hurt less worthy of healing.

Lastly, I give myself permission to be vulnerable and confront my abusers in order to find peace.

Practicing Forgiveness:

Feeling harmed by others oftentimes comes as a setback to our inner peace. How do we reclaim our joy? The act of forgiveness, unless we are fully evolved and enlightened, is not immediate. It requires time to fully understand and become aware of our pain and the stain it leaves on our psyche and our body. We need to sit with the discomfort before we can fully let go of the anger, disappointment, and hatred that the injury might have caused. It also takes time to honor the emotions—whether anger, fear, or sadness—that arose to protect us. Those emotions help us decide whether to fight back, freeze/do nothing, or flee/escape. Only after we have sufficiently sat with the pain should we begin the process of letting go.

Why should we even try to forgive? If nothing else, holding on to negativity keeps us in its energy, giving the evildoers continued power over us, beyond the first strike. Negative states consume and derail our energy, which then make us victims of our own inflicted harm and continues our cycle of pain. If we continue harboring these negative emotions beyond their expiration date, they can lead to reactive desires for grudge, revenge, and spitefulness. And ultimately, staying in the 'sunken spaces' of our mind takes us away from our true higher Self, and as detailed before, simultaneously harms our bodies.

To begin the act of forgiveness, it might be helpful to try practicing non-hatred, i.e. having no attachment to the feelings that were engendered. One way of getting there is to prioritize loving Self and not wanting to harm our Self by wasting precious karma on someone else's bad act. Getting to a neutral state in which the psychic charge has dissipated makes it easier to move toward loving kindness, forgiveness, and compassion for Self and towards others. For it is an act of self-compassion to not waste time dwelling in negative energy. It is also an act of compassion towards the other by understanding that by harming us, our offender has also harmed him or herself by leaving their own path of righteousness to inflict the harm.

We oftentimes experience much of our anguish in our relationships with others, especially those with whom we are intimately involved. This usually is a result of not dealing with our partner, as they are, how they show up. We tend to fixate upon them as our ideal construct of how we would like them to be. If our partner treats us with disrespect, if they do not want to be fully present with us in spite of our wanting to be with them, our focus should not be on "fixing" them. We should ask our Self if this is a relationship of mutuality and respect. Is this an affirmation of my self-worth and value, my Creator-bestowed right to dignity? Or am I, as was described by Dr. Irv Yalom in his discourse on the existential concept of isolation, merely using another to fend off loneliness.

Many a friendship or marriage has failed because, instead of relating to and caring for one another, one person uses another as a shield against isolation. A common and vigorous attempt to solve existential isolation is fusion—the softening of one's boundaries, the melting into another. Fusion eradicates anxiety in a radical fashion— by eliminating self-awareness. The person who has fallen in love and entered a blissful state of merger is not self-reflective because the questioning lonely "I" dissolves into the "we." This one sheds anxiety but loses oneself.

So whether the hurts turn up in our intimate relationships, in other relationships outside of our close circles, or with strangers whose actions have penetrated our sphere of being, forgiveness is ultimately about freeing one's Self from internalizing the negative energy of their bad actions or words. Leave them to wrangle with their own conscience if they have one, and/or with their creator if they believe in one.

Establishing Rituals:

Rituals help us to connect to the sacred in our ordinary and everyday life. When we participate in rituals we suspend the linearity of time. We bring past certitude into the present together with our dreams of the future. As such, rituals can help to bind our anxieties, especially anxieties that arise in regards to the uncertainty of our existence in the world—our journey from birth through death. Many indigenous cultures use rites of passage rituals to reverently mark key life transitions from birth through puberty and into the various stages of adulthood. At critical periods when we are in need of renewal and rebirth, rituals, especially if molded in nature, help us connect to the magical and extraordinary forces that surround and shape us.

I recall being present at a coming of age ritual in rural Zimbabwe. It revolved around an uncle teaching a young boy about the act of betrothal and sex, and a grandmother doing the same for the young woman. It culminated with grandma being present on the night of the marriage to ensure that the sexual act was properly performed! I oftentimes wonder if the retention of such sexual coming of age rituals from the motherland could have been helpful in controlling the HIV/AIDS epidemic in the Black diaspora? Could Grandma play a key role as a sexual health educator once again?

When rituals are carried out in communal settings, they can help to make us feel supported and give us a sense of belonging. These experiences can help alleviate the sadness that comes from disconnection and loss; or, on the other hand, energize the celebration of happiness that comes from connections and additions we acquire through partnership and birth. If nothing else, rituals bring us comfort—the comfort of feeling that there are others with the same understanding or desire to discover symbols that authenticate the experience of being alive. The second line and jazz funeral tradition in New Orleans is one such release where music and dance are used to celebrate the life of the departed, momentarily escape the pain of death, and connect the living who mourn.

Some questions to Self:
- *Do I have a community that I can turn to at times when I need to ritualize my joys and/or sorrows?*
- *Do I create personal rituals that make me more present and alive?*

Practicing Creativity:

Channeling and bringing forth that which is the expressive and imaginative residue of our DNA helps us to feel connected to the larger life force, the Qi. The creative process taps into our intuitive Self beyond the constraints of our ego, fears, and judgment and gives an outlet to that which is unbound and uncensored inside, freedom. Creativity can provide a space to temporarily transcend reality and find solutions to issues that bring us anxiety. Creativity rises up from the heart-space, transcends language, and connects us with each other.

Take music for example, the universal tongue, understandable to all humanity regardless of cultural language. It's a very important component of psychological resistance for the Black diaspora. Recall the purging of grief and envisioning of pathways to freedom that were embedded in our Negro Spirituals! Or the resistance to white supremacy pouring from the lyrics in the early days, before the commercial sell-out of reggae and hip-hop! Music is the language of our emotions, at times taking us to the deep recesses of feelings and memories we had long forgotten. Recall how transfixed and nostalgic we become when we hear an old song that had special meaning at some point in our lives.

Be it the visual, performing, or writing arts, creativity allows us to open and soften our hearts and allow that which is untethered and unknown within the human spirit to emerge. By helping us to push back against our fears of nothingness, creativity is a perfect antidote to feelings of personal and/or existential despair, hopelessness, and non-being. It frees us up to contemplate life and death simultaneously. Creative processes also bridle our schizoid tendencies and protect us from insanity by providing outlets for confusing and contradicting thoughts and feelings—getting it out on paper or working it out in movement.

Most important, creative processes help us to realize that we are at all times co-creating our lives—drawing, painting, writing, dancing, chanting, singing, and drumming the chapters of our biographies.

Some questions to Self:
- *What are my creative outlets?*
- *How do I allow myself to be free to be?*

Practicing Burnout Avoidance:

Empathy requires putting our Self in someone else's shoes, and compassion takes that even a bit further—noticing, feeling, and taking action to relieve someone else's suffering, AKA "empathy in action." For many Black people, empathy and compassion come easily. In spite of our religiosity, I have observed that very few of us have adopted the "eye for an eye" mentality. How else would we have gone on living with our oppressors all these years without retaliation against their terrorism? Imagine feeding our oppressors' child with the milk from our breast while our children went hungry! But in being empathic and compassionate with others, how do we avoid entering into their suffering?

The Buddhist nun Joan Halifax teaches that to avoid overexposure and taking on someone else's suffering, we should use contemplative practices to stabilize our boundaries, i.e. creating a balance between hyper-arousal and numbing withdrawal. If we suffer along with those we are attempting to help, we become useless and cannot help them. We need to recognize that their experience is theirs, not ours. The challenge is to figure out how to empathically support them in their distress and help without taking on their pain.

An important question to Self:
- *Do I personalize other people's suffering to the extent that I lose my footing in their sorrows, or do I create enough boundaries so that I have the strength to help them?*

Practicing Laughter, Imagination, and Play:

Play allows us to fall free, roll in the grass, run through the meadow, fill up and feast on happiness and pleasure, allowing our hearts to overflow with joy. Play releases us from fear and allows us to attach to more pleasurable states. As infants, it was the playfulness of our mother/caretaker that helped us to suspend the harsh realities of living and growing and instead become soothed by the pleasure that comes from playing. As toddlers, play was primarily focused on imitating adult behavior, which helped us develop mastery through manipulation and construction. Between the ages of three to six years old, engaging in fantasy pretend play and imagination began to concretize the awareness of our capacity to go beyond the limits of our reality-bound egos and create imaginal fantasies.

These are key developmental steps that taught us how to take initiative and create pleasure in our lives. Deliberately being able to create our own playful sense of direction and purpose protected us from drifting into guilt, callousness, and inhibition. Those childhood games of house, doctor, or school helped us to imagine adulthood without the constraints of its structured reality. By the age of seven years, when we were cognitively able to engage in more structured play, sports, and card games, we began learning how to become more reality bound, while at the same time experience the pleasure of competition.

As adults, play helps us to tap back into our childlike fantastical and playful innocence. Play helps us to release ourselves into purposeful unscripted diversion, amusement, or recreation and as such can enliven and brighten our mood. Such playfulness releases us from the tethers of productive work and allows us to balance our ego's response to our bodily need for pleasure with our social expectations. This "letting go" helps us to release stress, belly laugh, and relax. Adult play also helps us reconnect with those preverbal memories that laid the foundation for our intuitive Self.

Some questions to Self:
- *With whom do I lose myself in playful surrender?*
- *When was the last time I flew a kite?*

Practicing Ancestral Reverence/Minimizing Ancestral Trauma:

The spirits of the ancestors can serve as a tremendous source of calming, know-how, and inner peace. Finding solace in the memory of those who went before us, by asking for protection, guidance, or inspiration, can help reduce our existential anxieties about the mystery of life and death. We should honor and revere the memory of our ancestors by creating altars, pouring libations, invoking their presence in ritual or prayer, and/or making sacrifices. Knowing that we belong to those who came before us, and that they have walked these paths before us, can give us more space to create resilience.

Communal rituals that memorialize historical/ancestral traumas can be very releasing at the individual and collective level. It helps to put these acts of horror into the context of their time and place, at the same time energizing the determination and activism that ensures such things will never happen again. A prime example of this is the way in which Jewish culture memorializes the Holocaust with remembrance days and museums. The recent burgeoning of African American museums and other places of remembrance of slavery and colonization are a great start. Many more are needed!

A question to Self:
- *Indeed, if I believe that I am my ancestors' imagining of moving towards liberation, do I pay homage to the suffering of my ancestors that has now allowed me more freedom of being?*

Practicing Centering in Nature:

Mother Nature brings us up close and personal with the wondrous magnificence of the beauty of that which created life—God, Great Spirit, the universal unknown. The unexplainable awesomeness of a sunrise or sunset reminds us of the mystery of the universe, one that is unknown to our conscious being. Centering the little dot of our Self within the enormity of the vast surrounding universe brings a calming humility and reverence for the unknowable. Being connected to the duality inherent in nature, her destructive as well as creative forces, helps us to accept our own. Centering in nature helps us to appreciate and walk in the tension between the yin and yang that is life.

Mother nature can shed light on our true nature if we open ourselves up and revel in her raw beauty and aesthetics. She strips us bare to the core of our creation, just like the trees, the ocean, the mountains, and plains; they have no cover.

Some questions to Self:
- *How do I engage in and feel the mystery and magic of mother earth?*
- *Do I, and how often?*
  - ○ *Grow a garden—eat the fruits*
  - ○ *Walk barefooted on the earth*
  - ○ *Stroll through the woods, forest or park*
  - ○ *Stand under a waterfall*
  - ○ *Ponder the ocean's ebb and flow*
  - ○ *Sit by a river's edge*
  - ○ *Make sand castles at the beach*
  - ○ *Walk in the rain*
  - ○ *Climb / hike up a mountain*
  - ○ *Pick wild flowers or wild berries*

Practicing Rest:

An important, and oftentimes overlooked source of healing is rest. When our minds or bodies are damaged, the body has to work overtime. Rest allows the body to divert energy from other energy-consuming activities into the areas of increased need. Rest decreases heart and respiratory rates and decreases our nervous system's reactivity to external stimuli.

As a preventive measure, rest allows us to stop, look, listen, and sink into calmness. One sure way to get there is with mindful breathing focused on the outbreath. Those of us who are yoga practitioners know that the most important pose is shavasana, or the corpse pose. The repose helps our body integrate the healing that came from practicing the other poses. Often, in this state of relaxation, our creativity unfolds and ignites our innate intelligence. So do not worry about seeming lazy or unproductive when you are in such a state. Relax even more so that the fruits of your rest can contribute to the fruits of your labor.

The ultimate form of rest is sleep. It is so important to our wellbeing; going longer than three days without sleep can trigger manic episodes in some individuals. We need at least six to eight hours of good sleep per night. Sleep delivers our body to its innate healing energy. Research shows that poor sleep impairs the parasympathetic (soothing)/sympathetic (stimulating) balance and increase systemic inflammation as well as impairs glucose regulation. During sleep, all senses are quieted and shut down except for our hearing, perhaps to allow for the whisper of the dawn to beckon it is time to get "WOKE."

Some questions to Self:
- *Do I allow myself to get at least 6 hours of sleep per day?*
- *When I go on vacation, do I vacate and retreat, or do I fill up my time with activities?*

Chapter 14

The Revolution

Ultimately, healing is the dynamic process of recovering our sacredness. It requires releasing woundedness: all that which would otherwise stagnate our growth. The healing journey requires us to be vulnerable in the face of our pain and our joy and in the face of our unavoidable death. Healing the Black mind and body requires that we slow down, stop, look, listen, and trust that we can act from a place of deep knowing. Healing requires us to live from the space of as-is and deal with reality; not the space of as-if, where things are not as they are but how we want then to be.

All that is required is that we turn up with determination, dedication, and devotion to being the best that is available to us in any moment. Never mind being doubtful or afraid. It simply means that we know that there is so much that we do not know in any given moment, but trust that life will gradually unfold her mysteries—if we are open to their manifestation. Ultimately, we must have faith that what is will be.

Healing is traveling into the interior of our being and coming to know our truer Self, the one we have always desired to become. And when we go there, just maybe we will discover that this is where the life force resides in us and allow that knowledge to restore our confidence in that which we know to be our truth.

Healing mind, body, and spirit is a love journey back to the Self, a dance within the beauty and awe of the universe. The healing journey helps us discover our oneness with the divine and our connection to all beings. It is a lesson in learning how dependent we are on each other.

We maintain the healing journey by the continued commitment to our self-care. As previously discussed, self-care is the ongoing journey of deepening our self-discovery and nurturance of the true nature of our total being—physical, mental, and essence (spirit, soul).

We are not alone on this journey. Healing and ongoing self-care behoove us to move beyond our superficial boundaries to connect with all that the universe has surrounded us with: her plants, her animals, her oceans, her earth, and her sky. I invite you therefore to be on the journey of continuously contemplating how to compile a life of caring and compassion for your Self so that you can beam the same to others in your small circles and the larger universe!

Let's end with a simple devotion to Self:

Pour libations.
Drink wine.
Light candles.
Dance with the stars at night.
Sing to yourself in the shower.
Write a love letter to yourself!

Self-Care: Love Letter to ME

"Caring for my body, being aware of my mind, honoring my spirit is my lifelong dance with my divine."

Dear Me/_____,
I hereby affirm my devotion to continually optimize my physical, mental, and spiritual well-being. As a testament to my dedication to this lifelong journey of self-actualization, I hereby devote my entire being to:

For the following prompts, write simple self-loving steps you can take along the way.

Be kinder and gentler with myself. I will:

_____

_____

Be more honest with myself. I will:

_____

_____

Be more forgiving of myself. I will:

_____

_____

Relax more deeply. I will:

_____

_____

Have more fun. I will:

_____

_____

Experience the beauty of nature more frequently. I will:

_____

_____

Nurture my dreams more intentionally. I will:

_____

_____

Surrender to the mystery of my being more joyfully. I will:

_____

_____

And, as I strive to live more fully in the present moment I am practicing letting go of past regrets and future worries.

Signed _____

Date   _____

P.S. I promise to check up on how well I am doing at least once a month. I might even write myself another love note, as upon myself I dote.

NOTES

Caligor E, et al. *Psychodynamic Therapy for Personality Pathology: Treating Self and Interpersonal Functioning.* American Psychiatric Association Publishing, 2018.

Chae DH et al. "Racial Discrimination, Mood Disorders, and Cardiovascular Disease Among Black Americans." *Annals of Epidemiology*, vol. 22, no. 2, Feb. 2012, pp. 104-111.

Cobbs, Price M, Grier William H. *Black Rage.* Basic Books, 1968.

Crenshaw, Kimberle. "Mapping the Margins of Intersectionality." *Stanford Law Review*, vol. 43, Jul. 1991, pp. 1241 - 1299.

Cress Welsing, Francis. *The Isis Papers: The Keys to the Colors*, Third World Press, 1992.

Cronholm PF, Forke CM, Wade R, et al. "Adverse Childhood Experiences: Expanding the Concept of Adversity." *American Journal of Preventative Medicine*, vol. 49, no. 3, 2015.

DeGruy Leary, Dr. J. *Post Traumatic Slave Syndrome: America's Legacy of Enduring Injury and Healing.* Uptone Press, 2005.

Din-Dziethan et al. "Perceived Stress Following Race-Based Discrimination at Work is Associated With Hypertension in African–Americans. The Metro Atlanta Heart Disease Study, 1999–2001." *Social Science & Medicine,* vol. 58, no. 3, Feb. 2004, Pages 449–461.

Erikson, Erik H. *Childhood and Society.* WW Norton Pub, 1963.

Fanon, Frantz. *Black Skins, White Masks.* Grove Press Inc., 1968.

Felitti, V.J., et al. "Relationship of Childhood Abuse and Household Dysfunction to Many of the Leading Causes of Death in Adults. The

Adverse Childhood Experiences (ACE) Study." *American Journal of Preventive Medicine*, vol. 14, no. 4, 1998, pp. 245-258.

Fullilove M. *Root Shock: How Tearing Up City Neighborhoods Hurts America, and What We Can Do About It*. One World/Ballantine Books, 2004.

Fullilove M, Wallace R. "Forced Serial Displacement in American Cities 1916–2010." *Journal of Urban Health*, vol. 88, no. 3, Jun. 2011, pp. 381–389.

Geronimus, AT et al. "Weathering and Age Patterns of Allostatic Load Scores Among Blacks and Whites in the United States." *American Journal of Public Health*, vol. 96, no. 5, May 2006, pp. 826-833.

Gibran, Kahlil. *The Prophet*. Alfred A. Knopf, 1923.

Goodman, R.D., & West-Olatunji, C.A. "Traumatic Stress, Systemic Oppression, and rResilience in Post-Katrina New Orleans." *Spaces for Difference: An Interdisciplinary Journal*, vol. 1, no. 2, 2008, pp. 51-68.

Gollub E, Stein Z. "Living with Uncertainty: Acting in the Best Interest of Women." *AIDS Research and Treatment*, Epub Epub Article ID 524936, Nov. 1, 2012.

Gordon LR (ed). *Existence in Black: An Anthology of Black Existential Philosophy*. Routledge, 1997.

Halifax J. *Standing At The Edge: Finding Freedom Where Fear and Courage Meet*. Flatiron Books, 2018.

Harris-Perry, Melissa. *Sister Citizen: Shame, Stereotypes, and Black Women in America*. Yale University Press, 2013.

Hooks, bell. *Ain't I A Woman: Black Women; Black Women And Feminism*. South End Press, 1982.

Hunte H, et al. "Interpersonal Discrimination and Depressive Symptomatology: Examination of Several Personality-Related Characteristics as Potential Confounders in a Racial/Ethnic Heterogeneous Adult Sample." *BMC Public Health*, vol.13, no. 1084, 20 Nov. 2013.

Kanherkar et al. "Epigenetic Mechanisms of Integrative Medicine." *Evidence-Based Complementary and Alternative Medicine*. Vol 2017, Feb. 2017, Article ID 4365429. https://doi.org/10.1155/2017/4365429.

Katz M. "The Biological Inferiority of the Undeserving Poor." *Social Work and Society: International Online Journal*, vol. 11, no. 1, 2013.

Khomami, Nadia. "Michelle Obama Tells of Being Wounded by Racism as First Lady." *The Guardian*. https://bit.ly/2v3C9qb.

Lester, Neal, "It Takes a Village to Determine the Origins of an African Proverb." *NPR*, Jul. 2016, https://n.pr/2H7Zmvn.

"Making it Happen: A Guide to Delivering Mental Health Promotion." Department of Health and Social Care (UK). www. mentalhealthpromotion.net/resources/makingithappen.pdf

Mansfield B, Guthman J. "Epigenetic Life: Biological Plasticity, Abnormality, and New Configurations of Race and Reproduction." *Cultural Geographies*, vol. 22, no. 1, 2015, pp. 3-20.

Massey DS, Denton NA. *American Apartheid and the Making of the Underclass*. University of Chicago Press, 1993.

May, Rollo. *Love and Will*. Norton & Company, 1969.

McEwen BS. "The Brain on Stress: Towards and Integrative Approach to Brain, Body and Behavior." *Perspectives on Psychological Science,* vol. 8, no. 6, 2013, pp.673-675.

McEwen, BS. Allostasis and the Epigenetics of Brain and Body Health Over the Life Course." *JAMA Psychiatry,* vol. 74, no. 6, 2017, pp. 551-2018.

Metzl, Jonathan. *The Protest Psychosis; How Schizophrenia Became a Black Disease*. Beacon Press, 2010.

"Meet the Press." 1965. https://bit.ly/1ABoPl7

"The Nightly Show With Larry Wilmore: Black Fatherhood Keep it 100." *Comedy Central*. https://on.cc.com/2BcrjCX

"Five Years Later: Recovery From Post-Traumatic Stress and Psychological Distress Among Low-Income Mothers Affected by Hurricane Katrina." *Social Science & Medicine*, vol. 74, no. 2, Jan. 2012, pp. 150-157.

Prins et al. "The Primary Care PTSD Screener for DSM-5 (PC-PTSD-5): Development and Evaluation Within a Veteran Primary Care Sample."

Journal of General Internal Medicine, vol. 31, no. 10, Oct. 2016, pp. 1206-11.

Prevention Institute. "Adverse Community Experiences and Resilience: A Framework for Addressing and Preventing Community Trauma." Feb 2016. www.preventioninstitute.org/publications/adverse-community-experiences-and-resilience-framework-addressing-and-preventing

Raper, Arthur. *The Tragedy of Lynching*. University of North Carolina Press, 1933.

Roberts, Dorothy. *Killing the Black Body: Race, Reproduction, and the Meaning of Liberty*. Penguin Random House, Dec. 1998.

Roberts, Dorothy. *Fatal Invention: How Science, Politics, and Big Business Re-Create Race in the Twenty-First Century*. New Press, 2012.

Smiley, Calvin John & David Fakunle. "From 'Brute to 'Thug:' The Demonization and Criminalization of Unarmed Black Male Victims in America." *Journal of Human Behavior in the Social Environment*, vol. 26, no. 3-4, 2016, pp. 350-366.

Spitzer RL, et al. "A Brief Measure for Assessing Generalized Anxiety Disorder." *Archives of Internal Medicine*, vol. 166, no. 10, May 2006, pp. 1092-1097.

Spitzer RL, Williams JBW, Kroenke K, et al. "Utility of a New Procedure for Diagnosing Mental Disorders in Primary Care: The PRIME-MD 1000 Study." *Journal of the American Medical Association*, vol. 272, no. 22, 1994, pp. 1749–56.

Stahl SM. "Psychotherapy as an Epigenetic 'Drug': Psychiatric Therapeutics Target Symptoms Linked to Malfunctioning Brain Circuits With Psychotherapy as Well as With Drugs." *Journal of Clinical Pharmacy and Therapeutics*, vol. 37, 2012, pp. 249-253.

Sterling, P., and Eyer, J. "Allostasis: A New Paradigm to Explain Arousal Pathology." *Handbook of Life Stress, Cognition, and Health*. Edited by S. Fisher and J.T. Reason, Wiley, 1988.

Sterling, P. "Principles Of Allostasis: Optimal Design, Predictive Regulation, Pathophysiology and Rational Therapeutics." *Allostasis, Homeostasis and the Costs of Adaptation*. Edited by Jay Schulkin, Cambridge University Press, 2004.

Van der kolk, Bessel. *The Body Keeps the Score.* Penguin Books, 2014.

Walcot, Derek. *The Poetry of Derek Walcott 1948-2013.* Edited by Glyn Maxwell, Farrar, Straus and Giroux, 2014.

Wilkerson, Isabel. *Warmth of Other Suns: The Epic Story of America's Great Migration.* Vintage Books, 2011.

Wright, Robert. *Why Buddhism is True: The Science and Philosophy of Meditation and Enlightenment.* Simon and Schuster, 2017.

Yalom, Irvin D. *Love's Executioner and Other Tales of Psychotherapy.* Basic Books, 1989.

Yehuda R, Lehrner A, Bierer L. "The Public Reception of Putative Epigenetic Mechanisms in the Transgenerational Effects of Trauma." *Environmental Epigenetics*, vol. 4 no. 2, Jul 2018, pp1-7. https://doi.org/10.1093/eep/dvy018 eCollection 2018 Apr.